A **FLASHP●INTS** GAME

Raising the Eleventh Pillar

THE RATIFICATION DEBATE OF 1788

John Patrick Coby

SMITH COLLEGE

W. W. NORTON & COMPANY
Independent Publishers Since 1923

REACTING
TO THE PAST

W. W. Norton & Company has been independent since its founding in 1923, when William Warder Norton and Mary D. Herter Norton first published lectures delivered at the People's Institute, the adult education division of New York City's Cooper Union. The firm soon expanded its program beyond the Institute, publishing books by celebrated academics from America and abroad. By midcentury, the two major pillars of Norton's publishing program— trade books and college texts— were firmly established. In the 1950s, the Norton family transferred control of the company to its employees, and today— with a staff of five hundred and hundreds of trade, college, and professional titles published each year—W. W. Norton & Company stands as the largest and oldest publishing house owned wholly by its employees.

Copyright © 2021 by W. W. Norton & Company, Inc.
All rights reserved
Printed in the United States of America

First Edition

Editor: Justin Cahill
Project Editor: Linda Feldman
Editorial Assistant: Angie Merila
Managing Editor, College: Marian Johnson
Production Manager: Jeremy Burton
Media Editor: Carson Russell
Media Associate Editor: Alexander Lee
Media Project Editor: Rachel Mayer
Media Assistant Editor: Alexandra Malakhoff
Managing Editor, College Digital Media: Kim Yi
Ebook Production Manager: Sophia Purut
Marketing Manager, History: Sarah England Bartley
Design Director: Rubina Yeh
Designer: Jillian Burr
Director of College Permissions: Megan Schindel
Permissions Specialist: Josh Garvin
Photo Editor: Thomas Persano
Composition: Six Red Marbles
Illustrations: Mapping Specialists, Ltd.
Manufacturing: Sheridan Books, Inc.

Permission to use copyrighted material is included on page 141.

Library of Congress Cataloging-in-Publication Data

Names: Coby, Patrick, 1948- author.
Title: Raising the eleventh pillar : the ratification debate of 1788 / John
    Patrick Coby, Smith College.
Description: First edition. | New York, NY : W. W. Norton & Company, Inc.,
    [2021] | Series: Reacting to the past | Includes bibliographical
    references.
Identifiers: LCCN 2020032761 | **ISBN 9780393533033 (paperback)** | ISBN
    9780393533989 (epub)
Subjects: LCSH: Constitutional history—United States. | Virginia.
    Convention (1788) | United States—History—Confederation, 1783-1789.
Classification: LCC KF4541 .C545 2021 | DDC 342.7302/92—dc23
LC record available at https://lccn.loc.gov/2020032761

W. W. Norton & Company, Inc., 500 Fifth Avenue, New York, NY 10110
wwnorton.com
W. W. Norton & Company Ltd., 15 Carlisle Street, London W1D 3BS

1 2 3 4 5 6 7 8 9 0

John Patrick Coby is the Esther Booth Wiley 1934 Professor of Government at Smith College, where he teaches courses in political theory and American political thought. He is the author of six books and of numerous journal articles, book chapters, and book reviews. Included among his books are *Socrates and the Sophistic Enlightenment: A Commentary on Plato's Protagoras*; *Machiavelli's Romans: Liberty and Greatness in the Discourses on Livy*; and, in the Reacting to the Past series, *The Constitutional Convention of 1787: Constructing the American Republic*. At Smith he is the recipient of three teaching prizes: the Smith College Faculty Teaching Award, the Sherrerd Prize for Distinguished Teaching, and the Board of Trustees Honored Professor Award.

Contents

Raising the Eleventh Pillar

THE RATIFICATION DEBATE OF 1788

Part 1

Introduction

Brief Overview of the Game

Welcome to *Raising the Eleventh Pillar: The Ratification Debate of 1788*, a role-playing game in the Flashpoints series. In this game you will assume the role of a delegate to the New York State Ratifying Convention that met in the summer of 1788 to vote its acceptance or rejection of the Constitution drafted in Philadelphia the previous summer. Rather than learn of the event the traditional way, through lectures and exams, you will re-create the event yourselves, making history, so to speak, including the possibility of making an altogether different history, if that is your collective decision.

The delegates to the New York convention conducted a thorough review of the Constitution, but their focus, in the early going, was on the nature of democratic representation (and New York is chosen as the site of the game because its convention delved more deeply into this question than did any other state convention or even the delegates to the Constitutional Convention). That question—of democratic representation—is the chief issue at stake in this game.

A democracy is a form of government, or regime, in which the people rule themselves, without a king or a body of nobles lording over them. But what happens, when between the people and their laws, elected representatives are inserted, removing the people from direct involvement in the business of self-government? Is this regime still a democracy? If democracy is thus qualified by representation—and called sometimes **representative democracy**—how should representation be conceptualized, its purposes and conditions understood, for the resulting regime to be adequately democratic, if not fully so? What constitutional provisions are required to elect representatives who approximate the democratic ideal of the people governing themselves? Further, what provisions are required to keep such representatives faithful to their trust?

> **Representative democracy** was a common definition of a republic at the time. The term *republic*, as employed in this game, usually means a modified form of democracy.

But wait. This reasoning supposes that democracy is a good regime and that representative democracy is a satisfactory alternative, necessitated, most likely, by the size of the state. What, though, if democracy is a bad regime, made workable and acceptable only by the importation of nondemocratic elements? In that case, representation, as one of these nondemocratic elements perhaps, takes on an entirely different character; likewise, the qualities of the ideal representative are entirely different too, as are the restraints placed on the representative's actions.

As it happened, delegates to the New York State Ratifying Convention entertained both views of representation—that of a regrettable departure from democratic government and that of an essential corrective to democratic government. Accordingly, the debate among the delegates, or between the two parties that gathered in convention, went to the very heart of American democracy, investigating its advantages and its deficiencies. And as it happens, Americans today entertain both views, making the question of representation just as relevant in the twenty-first century as it was in the eighteenth.

While the game is about representation, the larger topic divides into seven subtopics, or issues. The game is built around these issues, proceeding through them one at a time, with votes taken on all but the first, and concluding with a vote to accept or reject the U.S. Constitution.

Your Part in the Game

You begin work by reading the short history that follows (see Historical Background on p. 6) and then by studying the respective positions adopted by the parties, the three stages of debate, and the structure and rules of the game (see Game Elements on p. 24). Your instructor will lead you through this material and, time permitting, through a discussion of the primary documents informing the game (see Core Texts on p. 46). Afterward, and before the game proper begins, the instructor will distribute the role sheets.

The roles are factional—Federalist, Antifederalist, and Moderate—and (if in use) individual—that is, named delegates to the convention. The faction role sheets are the same for all members of each faction. They tell you how to play the game, and they provide arguments for use in debate. Faction members decide among themselves who will take responsibility for which of the seven issues, which are presented in sequence in the faction role sheet. Each issue is accompanied by an explanatory paragraph that states the party's position and by a bibliography that identifies resources tailored to that issue. Some of these resources are found in the Core Texts in this game book and are available to all; some are known only to you, the speaker. Thus, when speaking, you can be better informed than other players, able to surprise and amaze! The Moderate faction is a special case, explained later in the game book. Individual roles include a character biography and additional game-play advice.

The game schedules (p. 42) tell you when an issue comes up for consideration—or when to be ready.

Ratification is a formal confirmation by a principal party (e.g., the people) of an action undertaken by an agent (e.g., a convention) and is a prerequisite of official adoption. While often a synonym for acceptance, ratification can also refer to the process of review and thus includes the possibility of nonratification, or rejection.

One game feature—a peculiarity of **ratification**—warrants advanced notice here, for it might easily mislead as to what it is you are doing when debating the Constitution. The feature is this: Whenever a body is charged with reviewing the work of another body, some comments will invariably take the form of objections, and some objections, if widely felt, will issue in calls for changes in the work. A body that changes, or amends, a work—the Constitution in this case—appears not to be ratifying (i.e., accepting or rejecting) but drafting its own replacement. That in fact is what happened to the delegates in New York. But the New York delegates were not writing a constitution (much to the consternation of some), and neither are you. Your comments then, formalized as votes, merely express the accumulating sense of the convention to approve or disapprove the Constitution, written already and by others, with the representation issue treated as a stand-in for the whole. More about this later.

Learning Objectives

Students playing the game should come to understand the following:

- The party alignments in place during the ratification debates and at the New York State Ratifying Convention.

- The two views of representation current at the time and still with us today.

- The interrelated character of constitutional provisions and the complexities and vagaries of group deliberations.

- The requirements, benefits, and drawbacks of democratic government.

Students also should make progress with such academic and life skills as:

- Persuasive writing.
- Public speaking, whether formally with speeches to the convention or informally in debate.
- Leadership, teamwork, and performance in a fast-paced and competitive environment.

 Historical Background

From Revolution to Constitution

The American Revolution waged against British rule proceeded along two fronts. First, there was fighting and a war to be won. General George Washington, commander of the Continental Army, was the primary actor here, though in an effort that enlisted the service of almost 300,000 men, not to mention the contributions and sacrifices of their families. Second, there was governance—of colonies, of states, and of a nation aborning—with more ink spilled than blood, but in rhetorical conflicts just as important to the outcome.

Wartime Governance

How did the colonies, later states, govern themselves, collectively, not individually, during the eight years of war (1775–83)[1] and the first years of peace, before the Constitution was written and sent to the states for their approval (1787–88)? More by happenstance than by design, it might be said.

In response to the Boston Tea Party (December 1773),[2] the British Parliament passed a package of laws known as the Coercive Acts; and in response to these laws, the thirteen colonies sent delegates to a meeting in Philadelphia to express their disappointment and displeasure (September–October 1774). The meeting came to be called the First Continental Congress; its successor, the Second Continental Congress, was scheduled for the following May.

This is where accident enters. For by the time the Second Continental Congress convened, fighting had already broken out at Lexington and Concord, Massachusetts (April 1775). Faced with the new reality of combat and the likelihood of more to come, the Second Continental Congress stayed in session as the effective wartime government of all the colonies; and one

---

1. Six years, not eight years, after the start of hostilities, major fighting ceased, following the British surrender at Yorktown in October 1781. The war though continued for another two years, until officially ended by the Treaty of Paris, signed in September 1783.
2. On the evening of December 16, 1773, Bostonians, disguised as Mohawk Indians, boarded three merchant ships loaded with tea and threw the cargo into the harbor. The British were not amused.

The central government operating under the Articles of Confederation was generally referred to as **Congress**.

of its first acts was to encourage the colonies to write their own constitutions, reorganizing themselves as independent states. The Second Continental Congress—the name often shortened to Continental Congress, or just **Congress**[3]—felt a similar need to establish its legal authority, which it did by writing a constitution for the nation, denominated the Articles of Confederation. The Articles was approved by Congress in 1777, but not until 1781 did it receive ratification by all the states (and unanimity was required). By March 1781 the American nation had its first constitution and its first legitimate government.

The Congress

How well did the Congress perform? It certainly had its defenders and champions, persons who appreciated the Articles' loose confederation of states, where most power was exercised locally. It also had its detractors. With no real taxing power, Congress was left to requisition (in essence, request) payments from the states, which as a rule were more unobliging than compliant; as a result, Congress was quite unable to raise funds sufficient to equip the army or pay down massive wartime debt. Congress could not effectively and exclusively regulate commerce between the states (which laid tariffs on each other) or between states and foreign countries. Congress could not enforce its laws, either because it had no enforcement power, as some suspected, or because enforcement required coercing whole states, not their individual citizens—and to coerce a state would likely mean war. And after the army was disbanded (largely unpaid), in November 1783, Congress could not protect the states against riot and insurrection. The alarm was sounded when debtors in western Massachusetts rose up in rebellion. This was Shays' Rebellion, occurring during the winter months of 1786–87. It convinced many that a tighter union with a stronger central government was essential.

---

3. As given in the Articles of Confederation, the full and formal title of this government was the "United States in Congress Assembled," abbreviated "Congress" in the document. By scholarly convention, the government after ratification of the Articles is sometimes called the Confederation Congress, to distinguish it from the government before ratification, called the Continental Congress.

The Constitutional Convention

Already plans were in place for a convention in the spring to amend the existing Articles.[4] Virginia led the way, and its delegation to the Constitutional Convention presented a plan of government on the third day after making a quorum. The Virginia Plan, so called, envisioned a national government divided into three branches (legislative, executive, judicial), its legislative branch divided into two chambers (lower and upper, later named House of Representatives and Senate), an executive empowered to veto legislation, nominate officials, command armies, etc., and an independent judiciary consisting of a supreme and appellate courts. The departure from the Articles was radical—no mere set of amendments was this proposal—for Congress then was a single-chambered body, the executive was mostly nonexistent, and the judiciary, far from independent, was routinely supplanted by the legislature.

Much of the early debate concentrated on representation in the Senate: would states be represented—have votes—proportionate to their populations, or would they possess equal votes as was presently the case? After a month of heated debate, the Convention decided on equal representation in the Senate, balanced against proportional representation in the House. The Great Compromise this was called.

But proportional representation, even if only in the House, meant that slavery became a national issue, for counting enslaved people in the represented population would augment the representation of some states (Southern states) at the expense of others (Northern states). The compromise here was to count slaves as three-fifths of free inhabitants and to lay taxes at the same rate. (Although the representation–taxation compromise, which also included commerce, addressed one aspect of the country's relationship with the institution of slavery, it did not address the more fundamental irony of a newly "freed" nation not granting freedom to a significant and growing population in chains. Some delegates did speak to this irony, but to little effect, because Southerners made it clear that their states would not join a union that put their plantation economies at risk.)

---

4. The lightly attended and unsuccessful Annapolis Convention, held in September 1786 for the purpose of regulating interstate trade, issued a call for a convention in May, which Congress and all the states heeded, except Rhode Island.

While these two extended debates were under way, the Convention intermittently took up the issue of the executive: how to elect the executive, or president, to what term of office, and whether the president would be eligible for reelection (among other issues). The Virginia Plan, after some revisions, specified election by the national legislature to a single, seven-year term. Though the proposal was reaffirmed several times in convention, an alternate plan gradually emerged, built around an electoral college as the electing body. The problem facing the delegates was this: a president elected by the national legislature and eligible for reelection would become the creature of the body that determined his fate. For the sake then of executive independence, a president must be confined to a single term. But a one-term president might abuse his powers before losing them or neglect the duties of his office if denied the chance of keeping it; at all events, the country would be deprived of continued use of his talents and experience. The electoral college seemed to be the solution to these difficulties. Because the college would be a temporary body, chosen just before the election and disbanded

Signing of the Constitution General Washington presides over the signing of the Constitution, while the delegates look on and wait their turn. This 1940 painting by Howard Chandler Christy was commissioned by Congress to commemorate the sesquicentennial of the Constitution. It hangs in the House wing of the U.S. Capitol.

thereafter, and because it would gather not in one place but in separate state capitals, it eliminated the danger of a sitting president, seeking reelection, bribing the legislature or being extorted by it. On recommendation by a committee, the Convention, close to its end, adopted the electoral college as the mode of electing the president.

Besides senatorial representation, slavery, and the organization of the executive—perhaps the three most contentious and complicated issues—the Convention debated myriad other constitutional provisions, too numerous to mention, much less discuss here.

Work on the Constitution was finally completed after nearly four months of painstaking deliberation. September 17, 1787, was the date when thirty-nine delegates to the Constitutional Convention put their names to the finished document. Three other delegates refused to sign, however, and their opposition was a warning that ratification might face a hard road ahead.

From Constitution to Ratification

Reception in Congress

The Constitution was taken north from Philadelphia by the Convention secretary, who on September 20 laid it before Congress, meeting in New York City. The Convention asked Congress to transmit the document to the states; Congress's endorsement, while welcome, was not required and, in the end, was not provided. Opponents in Congress objected: they cited the illegality of the Constitution (more than a set of amendments to the Articles of Confederation as authorized by Congress),[5] they complained of being rushed, and they wanted changes. But supporters were in the majority, many of whom had been members of the Convention. On September 28, after two days of debate, the parties agreed unanimously to transmission without recommendation, instructing state legislatures to submit the Constitution "to a convention of delegates, chosen in each state by the people thereof."

---

5. The letter of authorization from Congress stated that the Convention was to meet "for the sole and express purpose of revising the Articles of Confederation."

Early Reception in the States

Most states set to work immediately, with either their legislatures already in session and able to organize elections for ratifying conventions or with their governors willing to call special sessions of the legislatures to accomplish the same. Pennsylvania provided the most interesting case. Its legislature was then in session, meeting in the same building that hosted the Constitutional Convention (Philadelphia's State House, later renamed Independence Hall). The legislature, though, was set to adjourn on September 29. Being so near the business of constitution making, it was the first to see the text of the Constitution (on the 19th, printed in the *Pennsylvania Packet*). But not until the document had traveled to New York and returned with Congress's blessing, could the legislature authorize a ratifying convention. On the 29th, by express rider, the Constitution arrived back at the State House. With only hours to spare, the legislature set November 6 as the date for elections and November 21 as the start date of its convention. In Georgia a special session of the legislature was called by the governor for September, but it made a quorum only in October. It set December 4 as the date for elections and December 25 as the start date of a convention.

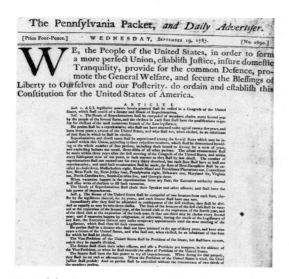

Text of the Constitution, *Pennsylvania Packet* The *Pennsylvania Packet* was the first newspaper to print the full text of the proposed Constitution. Other newspapers would soon do the same.

Reception in New York

The pattern of eager legislatures and governors scheduling quick elections and conventions was broken in New York, however. For the governor of New York, George Clinton, was a known, if undeclared, adversary of the Constitution. New York waited until January 1788 when the next regular meeting of the legislature was scheduled to convene. The delay was calculated on the governor's part: linger and assess; hope that ratification would fail elsewhere and the issue would just fade away, without offense given or enemies made. But as of January, the results were positive in all states—five of them thus far (see the Chronology on p. 22). The issue wasn't going away, and New York would have to declare itself willing or unwilling to call a convention.

As it turned out, opposition to a ratifying convention proved negligible; the only points of contention were whether the legislature's instructions would include a censure of the Philadelphia Convention for having exceeded its authority and whether the right of proposing amendments would be explicitly stated. The motions lost on mostly close votes in both chambers, whereupon both chambers, by comfortable margins, approved the original proposal, which was to schedule elections for April and a ratifying convention for June.

The Newspaper War

But the citizens of New York, at least those of a literary bent, were not so patient as to wait until spring before being heard on the subject. The newspaper war began much earlier. Opening shots were fired in the summer of 1787 while the Convention still sat. These were of a personal nature with charges of usurpation and demagoguery hurled back and forth.

The more serious fighting arose after arrival of the Constitution in late September. The first entry, writing for the opposition, was "Cato," widely suspected to be Clinton himself. Cato warned against consolidated union on a continental scale, as this would require despotic power at the center to hold the disparate parts together. Effective government over a large territory would threaten liberty, Cato argued, while ineffective government would tempt insurrections destructive of peace. Cato was answered by "Caesar," widely suspected to be Alexander Hamilton, who had started the verbal fisticuffs with an attack on Clinton in July. Caesar prophesied darkly that General Washington would either serve as president of a united country or as generalissimo in a divided one. For if the Constitution failed, the country would split into separate, quarreling confederacies, each prioritizing its own defense against distrusted neighbors. Supporting Caesar were "Americanus," "A Citizen of Philadelphia," "Giles Hickory," "Rough Carver," and "Timon," with essays published mainly in *The New-York Daily Advertiser*. Supporting Cato were "Cincinnatus," "A Countryman," "A Republican," "Expositor," "Rough Hewer," and "Columbian Patriot," with essays published mainly in *The New-York Journal*. The moderate middle had its representative in a writer aptly named "Medium." The wits also chimed in, adopting pseudonyms like "Roderick Razor" and "One of the Nobility," and authoring satirical doggerel like the "Newsmonger's Song," which read in part:

> Come on brother scribblers 'tis idle to lag,
> The Convention has let the cat out of the bag,
> Write something at random, you need not be nice,
> Public Spirit, Montesquieu, and great Dr. Price
>   Down, down, down, derry, down.
>
> Talk of Holland and Greece, and of purses and swords
> Democratical mobs and congressional lords;
> Tell what is surrendered, and what is enjoy'd,
> All things weigh alike, boys, we know, in a void
>   Down, down, down, derry, down.[6]

While partisan skirmishing occupied the lesser combatants, the main battle, involving detailed explication of the text of the Constitution,[7] was carried on by the three big guns: "Publius," writing *The Federalist* in support of the Constitution; "Brutus" and "The Federal Farmer," writing eponymous essays in opposition. The big guns supplied the arguments, their minions added the venom.

Preparing for the April election meant taking account of certain political facts on the ground. As of 1788, the settled portions of New York State were divided into thirteen counties (plus one in the process of being organized). The southern counties consisted of New York (Manhattan), Richmond (Staten Island), Kings (Brooklyn), Queens (central Long Island), Suffolk (eastern Long Island), and Westchester (Bronx and above). Upcountry from

---

6. Quoted in Clarence E. Miner, *The Ratification of the Federal Constitution by the State of New York* (New York: Columbia University Press, 1921), p. 71.
7. The text of the Constitution is provided in the appendix (p. 131).

these, and filling the Hudson River Valley, were Orange, Dutchess, Ulster, Columbia, Albany, Washington, and Clinton (named after the governor and just carved out of Washington at the top of the state but voting with Washington for now). The one, great western county, geographically as large as all the others combined and reaching to the Finger Lakes region, was Montgomery (previously called Tryon after the last colonial governor).

Politically the state divided between the commercial counties in the south, including the trading towns along the Hudson River, and the agricultural counties in the north, including much of Long Island. The former wanted a stronger union able to collect taxes, pay down debt, open up markets, and enforce treaties; the latter wanted a weak(ish) union, like that which existed under the Articles of Confederation, since the current arrangement allowed New York to retain most of its sovereign independence. Going it alone these past several years, New York had recovered nicely from the

The Battle Is Joined The essays of Publius and Brutus, and other controversialists of the day, first appeared in local newspapers, printed in small type and narrow columns, and often sharing space with news stories, announcements, and advertisements.

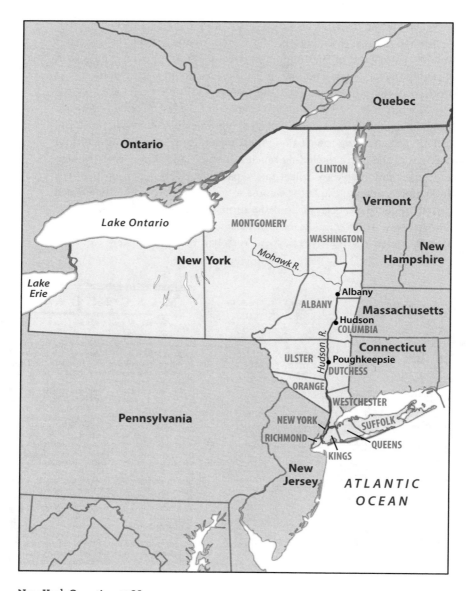

New York Counties, 1788

war, because impost fees, paid by merchants in neighboring states using the New York port, kept taxes low for residents and coffers full for the government. Governor Clinton put together the system and was popular with voters because of it. The worry though was that an invigorated national government with power over interstate commerce would bring an end to these discriminatory practices. Nevertheless, New York could not realistically hope to stand apart, not against the other states united under a new charter of union. New York was at liberty to decide on its own participation but could hardly prevent the participation of others.

The January legislature that agreed to schedule elections for April also agreed that the thirteen-plus counties would send the same number of delegates to the ratifying convention as they sent to the state assembly. The assembly had sixty-five delegates, and so the convention would have sixty-five too. These would be allotted in proportion to county population, and elections for assembly and convention would occur at the same time.

Both sides felt that they held the upper hand. Proponents of the Constitution, called Federalists, had the immense prestige of the Constitution's framers to draw on and widespread trepidation about the consequences of failure; they also had friendly postmasters willing to delay delivery of the opposition's mail. Opponents, called Antifederalists (see later for more on the names), had the popularity of the governor, the jealousy of state officials anxious to protect the importance of their local offices, and a change in the New York election law that extended the franchise to property-less males age twenty-one and older. Another practice, if not law per se, permitted candidates to stand for election in multiple counties. Thus prominent oppositionists on the ballot in hostile New York City, where they had little chance of success, were also on the ballot in hospitable upstate counties, where their elections were ensured. Such was true for Clinton, running in both New York and Ulster counties and successful only in the latter.

The Election Campaign

The campaign through the winter and spring months was boisterous, tenacious, and something less than fully principled. A fake letter and fake reply were published purporting to be from and to a distinguished Pennsylvania framer. The framer laid out a strategy for success, and his New York correspondent commented dolefully on the strength of the opposition. The Pennsylvanian coached: take over the press, misrepresent public opinion, exaggerate support, and promise offices to the well-to-do. And the New Yorker grumbled in reply: the merits of the argument are all on the other side, our underhanded tactics were spared exposure only by a quick victory elsewhere, and the people here are incorruptible and dare to think for themselves. Scribblers and operatives were alike engaged. Much was at stake, causing passions to run high, turn heated, and become enflamed—as happened to copies of the Constitution, burned in Orange and Ulster counties. And during July 4 celebrations, while the convention met, actual fighting erupted in Albany, with bayonets and swords, costing the life of one and leaving eighteen others injured (though reports varied); prisoners were taken and later released.

Violence of another sort occurred as well. Shortly before the April voting was set to begin, the so-called Doctors' Riot swept across New York City. A young boy, peering through a window of the city hospital, saw a medical student severing the limb of a cadaver. The medical student, seeing the curious boy, waived the severed arm aloft, declaring that it belonged to his mother—just deceased, as it happened! The boy, terrified, ran screaming to his father. The father, in a white-hot rage, gathered up neighbors and attacked the hospital, destroying instruments, threatening staff, and collecting what body parts they could find for burial. The authorities removed doctors and students to the jail for safe keeping. The next morning and afternoon, a larger crowd, numbering 2,000, rioted through the streets and stormed the jail. A party of leading citizens tried guarding the building, but they were overwhelmed by a hail of bricks. John Jay, secretary of foreign affairs, was struck in the forehead and grievously injured. The

CONVENTION DEMONSTRATIONS

Other conventions had their moments of excitement too. A fistfight broke out in the Massachusetts convention when Elbridge Gerry presumed to address the assembly in person. Gerry had been a delegate to the Constitutional Convention and was one of the three who had refused to sign the document. That refusal made him unpopular in Massachusetts and cost him election to the ratifying convention. But he was permitted to attend sessions to explain his decision, on condition that he confine himself to written responses to direct questions. He did not, and a brawl ensued. Likewise, Pennsylvania descended into farce when two opposition members, who had gone into hiding to prevent the legislature from making a quorum, were kidnapped and forcibly returned to the chamber so that the legislature, with its quorum in place, could set the date for a ratifying convention.

governor was forced to call out the militia. Three were killed and many more wounded.

By comparison, the election that month was a tame, if pell-mell, affair. Without formal parties in place, the nominating process was determined on the run. Individuals and citizen groups, hiding behind pseudonyms, published lists of candidates in local newspapers for consideration by readers. Such lists began appearing in February and proliferated thereafter. Some order was imposed in April and in the city, when the Federalist campaign committee, the New York City Federal Committee, offered its own list, promoted by repeated publication, broadsides, and a poetic mnemonic:

> Mr. [John] Jay, Col [Alexander] Hamilton, [Richard] Harrison, [Nicholas] Low,
> Are honest, good patriots all of us know;
> Mr. [Robert] Livingston, [Isaac] Roosevelt, his Worship the Mayor [James Duane],
> Will look to your interests with very great care.
> Judge [Richard] Morris and [John Sloss] Hobart are true to the cause,
> They'll preserve us from ruin by strength'ning our laws.[8]

Endorsement by some of the city's ethnic and trade associations (Germans in the former category, and carpenters and mechanics in the latter) gave the list a semi-official status.

The Anti-Federal Committee, centered in Albany, appended a list of endorsed candidates to its party platform, titled "A Manifesto of a Number of Gentlemen from Albany County," that cataloged the committee's many objections to the Constitution. Ulster County Antifederalists staged a rally in one town and convened a meeting of district representatives in another to settle on its list. Other counties, to varying degrees, followed this pattern.

Dirty tricks were not out of the question: Antifederalists in New York City submitted a counterfeit Federal Committee list with Governor Clinton's name included; and Federalists in Ulster nominated a phony list of Antifederalist candidates to confuse the voters.

---

8. Quoted in Linda Grant De Pauw, *The Eleventh Pillar: New York State and the Federal Constitution* (Ithaca, NY: Cornell University Press, 1966), pp. 153–54 (with alterations). The names are of all nine Federalist candidates running in New York City.

Voters cast their votes by ballot (a recent innovation in the state)[9] for as many candidates as there were delegates allotted to the county. Candidates ran on party tickets.

Voting in late April extended over four days and into early May. Delivery, tabulation, and reporting of the votes extended into early June. The result, once in, was a decisive victory for the Clinton faction, which carried all but four counties and which returned more than two-thirds of the delegates, 46 to 19. No county split its delegation,[10] and the margins of victory were quite high in most. The tally is shown in the table below.

Much of the reason for the Antifederalist landslide was an increase of votes and voters for convention delegates as compared to assemblymen

RESULTS OF THE NEW YORK VOTE

COUNTY	ALLOTTED DELEGATES	WINNING PARTY	WINNING PERCENTAGE
Albany	7	Antifederalist	64%
Columbia	3	Antifederalist	55.5%
Dutchess	7	Antifederalist	66.5%
Kings	2	Federalist	(returns unrecorded)
Montgomery	6	Antifederalist	60%
New York	9	Federalist	98%
Orange	4	Antifederalist	100%
Queens	4	Antifederalist	55%
Richmond	2	Federalist	(returns unrecorded)
Suffolk	5	Antifederalist	(returns unrecorded)
Ulster	6	Antifederalist	98%
Washington and Clinton	4	Antifederalist	(returns unrecorded)
Westchester	6	Federalist	63.5%

9. Article VI of the New York State Constitution of 1777 invited the legislature, after the war, to experiment with ballot voting in place of voice voting (*viva voce*). The purpose and expected benefit was to better "preserve the liberty and equal freedom of the people." On February 13, 1787, the legislature approved ballot voting for senators and assemblymen, having approved the same for governors and lieutenant governors nine years earlier.

10. For example: all nine candidates recommended by the New York City Federal Committee were elected, as were all seven candidates recommended by the Albany County Anti-Federal Committee.

(concurrent elections), whether because of property qualifications still in place for the latter, spoiled ballots, or the inconvenience of standing in line a second time. But what seemed like a one-party blowout was tempered by the fact that many of the Antifederalist delegates were soft in their allegiance, hesitant to reject the Constitution outright and hopeful that some accommodation might be reached.

Chronology

September 17, 1787	Constitution of the United States is signed in Philadelphia.
September 19	First copies of Constitution are printed by *Pennsylvania Packet and Daily Advertiser,* Philadelphia.
September 20	Constitution is received by Congress in New York City.
September 27	First letter by Antifederalist "Cato" is published.
September 28	Congress votes to transmit Constitution to thirteen states.
October 1	First letter by Federalist "Caesar" is published.
October 8	First letter by Antifederalist "Federal Farmer" is published.
October 18	First letter by Antifederalist "Brutus" is published.
October 27	First paper by Federalist "Publius" is published.
December 7	Delaware ratifies (30–0).
December 12	Pennsylvania ratifies (46–23).
December 18	New Jersey ratifies (38–0).
December 21	Yates and Lansing write letter to Clinton explaining their reasons for leaving Constitutional Convention.
January 2, 1788	Georgia ratifies (26–0).
January 3	Connecticut ratifies (128–40).
January 11	New York State Legislature convenes.

February 6	Massachusetts ratifies (187–168).
February 22	New Hampshire convention adjourns until June.
April 26	Maryland ratifies (63–11).
May 26	South Carolina ratifies (149–73).
June 2	Virginia Ratifying Convention begins session.
June 17	New Hampshire Ratifying Convention begins session.
June 17	New York State Ratifying Convention begins session.
June 19	New York State Ratifying Convention resolves itself into committee of whole.

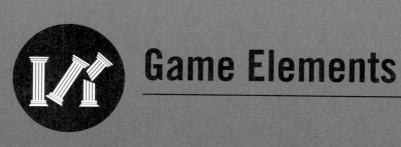

Part 3

Game Elements

Setting

You sit as delegates to the New York State Ratifying Convention, called by Governor George Clinton to accept or reject the Constitution drafted in Philadelphia the previous summer. The time is June–July 1788; the place is the Poughkeepsie courthouse, Dutchess County, New York, in the Hudson River Valley.

Eight states have ratified to date; nine are needed to give effect to the Constitution. But it matters which nine ratify, and without New York, which separates New England from the mid-Atlantic states, no viable union will form.[1] At least that's what some New Yorkers say—those hostile to the Constitution or merely neutral and wanting not to be hurried into ratifying. Those friendly to the Constitution caution that if New York takes too long to ratify, or rejects altogether, it will lose out on the chance of having the nation's new capital located in the state. Meanwhile, two other states, New Hampshire and Virginia, are currently in convention, racing to be the ninth state that puts the Constitution over.

A Boston newspaper, *The Massachusetts Centinel* (later joined by the *Independent Chronicle*), uses the metaphor of pillars of the federal government to symbolize the ratifying states. Starting in January of 1788, the *Centinel* publishes a series of woodcut engravings showing the multiplying lineup of pillars, usually with the hand of Providence extending from a cloud, lifting the latest one into place. (See the series of images, "Pillars of the Federal Edifice," on the following two pages.) If New Hampshire or Virginia ratifies as the ninth state and the other as the tenth, then New York, when ratifying, will become the ELEVENTH PILLAR in the colonnade.

---

1. The country divided into three regions of four states each: the New England states of New Hampshire, Massachusetts, Rhode Island, and Connecticut, called the Eastern states; the Middle states of Pennsylvania, New Jersey, Delaware, and Maryland; and the Southern states of Virginia, North Carolina, South Carolina, and Georgia. (Maryland was sometimes counted among the Southern states.) New York was a geographic outlier, not Eastern, not Middle, and blocking movement between the two. Says historian Clinton Rossiter: "some ratifications were absolutely necessary to win; just any nine were not enough to bring the Constitution to life. Any of at least four states—Massachusetts, New York, Pennsylvania, and Virginia—was in a physical and political position to wreck the whole scheme by holding out" (*1787: The Grand Convention* [New York: Norton, 1966], p. 279).

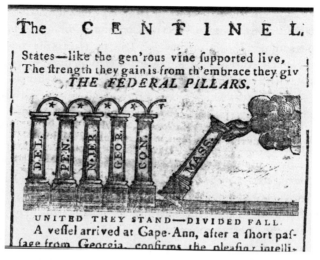

Five Pillars January 16 engraving depicting the pillars of the first five states to ratify, with the pillar of Massachusetts rising to make the sixth. Published in *The Massachusetts Centinel*, Boston.

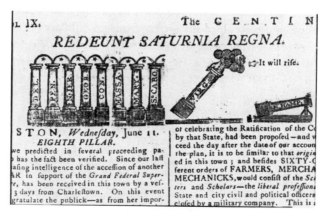

Eighth Pillar June 11 engraving depicting the pillar of South Carolina as the eighth state to ratify, with Virginia, in session ahead of New Hampshire, expected to ratify as the ninth. Published in *The Massachusetts Centinel*, Boston.

Ninth Pillar June 26 engraving depicting the pillar of New Hampshire as the ninth state to ratify, with Virginia expected to ratify as the tenth and New York as the eleventh. Published in the *Independent Chronicle and Daily Advertiser*, Boston.

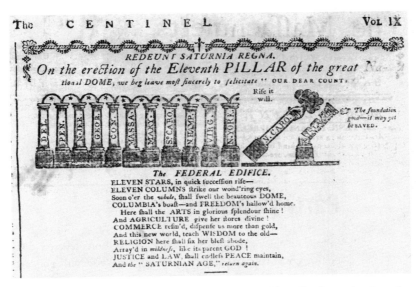

Eleventh Pillar August 2 engraving celebrating New York's ratification as the eleventh pillar in the federal colonnade, with the pillar of North Carolina rising into place as the twelfth, but with the crumbling pillar of Rhode Island casting doubt on the prospects of a thirteenth pillar being added to the colonnade. Published in *The Massachusetts Centinel*, Boston.

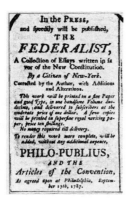

Order Your *Federalist* Now! In this advertisement for the forthcoming publication of *The Federalist*, "Citizen of New York" was listed as the pseudonymous author because James Madison from Virginia had not yet joined the project. "Philo-Publius" was William Duer.

Friends of the Constitution go by the name of Federalists, opponents by the name of Antifederalists.

These party labels have an interesting and contested history, caused by the fact that the word *federal* carries nearly opposite meanings. For *federal* can refer to a style of union based more on faith (*fides*) than on force; in that case *federal* is synonymous with *confederal* (with faith), and the union so formed is a confederation. Or *federal* can refer to the central government that oversees the confederation and to which the contracting parties (the states) send their delegates—as with the Continental Congress of the Articles of Confederation. After the war persons wanting to enhance the supervisory powers of Congress sometimes called themselves federalists; while those wanting to defend the independence of the states sometimes *were called*—they didn't call themselves this—antifederalists. The labels, however, did not take hold until a publisher brought out a collection of the newspaper essays by Publius under the title *The Federalist*, forcing the other side to accept the label Antifederalist. In a moment of exasperation, one Antifederalist spokesman asked plaintively if his interlocutor "would be complaisant enough to exchange names with those who dislike the Constitution, as it appeared . . . that they were federalists, and those who advocated it were anti-federalists."[2]

Some of you in the game will be Federalists, some Antifederalists, and some undecided Moderates.

Party Positions

While delegates to the New York convention debated dozens of constitutional issues, in this game you will concern yourselves with only one issue, or set of issues—namely, the

---

2. Melancton Smith at the New York State Ratifying Convention, June 20; in Jonathan Elliot, ed., *The Debates of the Several State Conventions on the Adoption of the Federal Constitution as Recommended by the General Convention at Philadelphia, in 1787*, vol. 2, 2nd ed. (Burt Franklin, 1888), p. 224.

qualities and obligations of **representatives** and the structural elements needed to elect and control them. Popular government in a country the size of America cannot operate as a direct democracy where the people assemble to pass laws of their own creation. Representation, all concede, is required; but whether as an unfortunate necessity of size, or as an instrument of enlightened lawmaking, is a question that divides the parties. Antifederalists incline toward the former view, Federalists toward the latter.

Representative has both a specific and a general meaning. Specifically, it refers to a member of the House of Representatives; generally, it refers to any member of Congress, senators included. In this game the term often encompasses both types of elected officials.

Antifederalists

Indeed, much of what divides and defines the parties is encapsulated in the representation debate. Antifederalists, as a rule, are distrusting of power. They think of government as a voracious monster devouring the property and liberties of ordinary citizens. Government is necessary for stability and security, they acknowledge, but government becomes an oppressor unless carefully watched and circumscribed. That is so because government reflects the character of its officers, persons ambitious for power, wealth, and status. Corrupt human nature is what makes governance so intractable a problem ("if we presume [that all men are dishonest], we shall be on the safest side," confessed one Antifederalist[3]), and representative democracy provides at best an imperfect remedy. Antifederalists seek, therefore, to elect officials who resemble the people in opinions, passions, and interests; for representatives who are *of* the people—the thinking goes—will be less prone to betray the public trust. Also, and as a precaution, Antifederalists seek to tighten the bonds that tie representatives to their constituents. The true representative is an **agent** of the people.

SIZE OF THE UNION The population at the time was about 3,500,000 (as determined by the 1790 census). It was less than half that of Great Britain but spread over a territory more than four times as large (Maine to Georgia). Contemporaries routinely described the United States as an empire. (Primary sources in the Core Texts sometimes put the population at 3,000,000.)

Antifederalists espouse the **agent** theory of representation. The theory posits that elected officials are responsible for carrying out the wishes of their constituents, and that officials are worthy of trust to the extent they share with their constituents the same backgrounds, experiences, and life circumstances.

---

3. June 25; ibid., p. 315.

Federalists and Antifederalists agree that the lower house is the people's house and so should be popularly elected.

Disagreement comes with the following Antifederalist positions and proposals (these are further elaborated in the faction role sheets, about which see later in the game book):

1. Representatives who are like the people represented, operating as their agents.

2. Increased size of the lower house, called the House of Representatives. (The Constitution calls for sixty-five representatives at the start, with expected growth to occur following censuses every ten years. But one representative per 30,000 inhabitants is the maximum that is ever allowed, and the beginning number of sixty-five—for a country of about 3,500,000—comes to a ratio closer to one representative per 54,000 inhabitants.)

3. Small electoral districts, the better to ensure election of candidates near to the people they represent.

4. Shorter terms and more frequent elections. ("Where annual elections end, tyranny begins," says the celebrated Montesquieu.)

5. Rotation of representatives, meaning term limits, or mandatory removal after a specified time in office and re-eligibility only after a specified time away.

6. Recall of representatives whose performances offend or disappoint— hence no fixed terms of office that are truly fixed.

7. Instructed voting, with the instruction coming from state legislatures, most likely.

This last provision reveals an additional Antifederalist conviction— namely, that government is dangerous to the degree that government is distant from the people. State government, being closer to the people, is safer than national government and can work to protect the people's liberties from encroachments by the national power. Liberty is local—i.e., is exercised and guarded locally—whereas power gravitates to the center. Power and liberty are enemies locked in eternal battle. National representatives are wont to shift their loyalties to the more important central government; they therefore require close supervising by governments back home.

Federalists

Federalists do not exactly disagree with their opponents' assessment of human nature: people are selfish, foolish, and intemperate, Federalists concede, and power mostly aggravates these failings of character. One Federalist puts the matter this way: "Men will pursue their interests. It is as easy to change human nature as to oppose the strong current of the selfish passions. A wise legislator will gently divert the channel, and direct it, if possible, to the public good."[4] But an attitude of constant suspiciousness toward those holding office is unwarranted, Federalists say, because officeholders come from the people (i.e., are not members of a permanent ruling class of hereditary nobles), serve at the people's pleasure, for limited periods of time, and are removable through the instrument of elections. Moreover, human beings are unequal in their talents, and it is a measure of a well-constructed government that talented individuals are drawn to its service. Their ambition can be a laudable motive and a public utility—not a mark of corruption—if rewards are paid them for promotion of the common good. The people may be honest, but they are rarely wise. If they wish to have the benefit of their leaders' wisdom, some degree of independence must be accorded these leaders—who are, again, elected officials answerable to the people. And if the common good is both national and local, then independence will allow elected officials the freedom to consider issues from a wider perspective than that of the states. The true representative is not of the people, but of the elite—sometimes called the "natural aristocracy"—because, being superior to the people, the true representative can better serve their needs. The true representative is a **trustee** of the public interest.

> Federalists espouse the **trustee** theory of representation. The theory posits that elected officials are responsible for enlightening public opinion, not simply reflecting it—the purpose being better deliberation regarding problems of national import.

Federalists, therefore, have in mind a different sort of representative operating under a looser set of restrictions. Federalists propose:

1. Representatives who are trustees of the common good, refining and enlarging public views.

2. A lower-house size large enough to be representative (if only somewhat) and small enough to be competent and efficient.

4. Alexander Hamilton, June 25; in Elliot, *The Debates of the Several State Conventions*, p. 320.

3. Election in large electoral districts, the better to secure election of the talented few.

4. Longer terms of office than the Montesquieuian norm: two years for lower house members, six years for upper house members.

5. Indefinite re-eligibility as a reward for service performed.

6. Fixed terms of office not subject to recall, lest independence be compromised.

7. Representatives free to vote as their opinions and consciences dictate— independence again, this time allowing for judgments shaped by the views and needs of the larger community.

Federalists challenge the notion that liberty is best protected at the local level. For local politics, they reason, will reflect the selfish wishes of mostly uniform local majorities (e.g., farmers, artisans, debtors), endangering the liberties of outvoted local minorities. Conversely, majorities that form at the national level, being coalitions of diverse interests (e.g., northern merchants, southern planters, western homesteaders), are likely to be more moderate in the objectives they pursue, because diverse coalitions will with difficulty come together around policies that are narrowly self-interested.

The Debate

The game debate will unfold in three phases, spread over two or three classes (see Game Schedules on p. 42).

First Phase

During the first phase, delegates will discuss **the characteristics desired in a representative**.

Should a representative, for example, be someone with superior intellect, education, and experience, able to analyze difficult problems and devise workable and acceptable solutions; someone additionally with the rhetorical skills to persuade and the personal charisma to lead? Or should integrity be the primary requirement: a decent, honest, straight-talking person who is true to his word; also a compassionate person able to commiserate with others? And should the likely wearing away of this basic human goodness under the corrupting influence of power be the primary concern? Is politics better practiced by people who *know how* or by people who *mean well*? And even allowing that both attributes are wanted in a representative, are they really that compatible, or must a choice be made, or at least a prioritizing of facilities and qualities?

Second Phase

During the second phase of the debate, delegates will propose means for securing the election of desirable characters to office.

One such means is the **size of the chamber**. Should it be large so as to represent all the interests and occupations contained in the country, aiming for an officialdom that replicates the populace? That way people will have confidence in their government, obey laws more gladly, and feel less the whip of coercive power. But is it possible, in a country bigger than a city-state, to represent every difference so completely? And is it necessary? Does one have to be a mechanic in order to represent mechanics? Maybe not. And maybe representativeness should not be the determining factor but instead the number of persons capable of fruitful deliberation. A large chamber is a chaos unless order is imposed. A large chamber may seem more democratic than a small chamber, but a large chamber will in fact be less democratic if, because of its size, a tight group of leaders is required to manage its business.

The greater the number of elected officials the smaller the electoral districts in which they are elected (unless elections are at-large and statewide).[5] The **size of the electoral district** is therefore a second means of shaping the character of representatives. A small size is a good thing, say some, because it puts ruler and ruled in closer contact, making accountability truly possible; and it is a good thing because it increases the chances of election

---

5. An at-large election is one in which the whole of the voting population, however demarcated (by state, by county, by municipality), serves as the electoral body. For example, a state would be conducting an at-large election for its, say, four congressional representatives, if all four were elected statewide, rather than separately in four electoral districts, where only the residents of those districts were voting. The Constitution allows states to make these decisions (Article I.4.1), though an act of Congress (1967) now requires that election of representatives occurs in single-member districts, geographically divided.

of middle-class persons outside the ranks of the country's elite. Others say that small electoral districts are a bad thing because they give prominence to demagogues practicing the low arts of calumny, vote buying, and haggling.

Third Phase

No method is foolproof. Scalawags and dunderheads will just as often win election as virtuous patriots and enlightened statesmen. How to guard against their misconduct and folly is the topic then of the third phase of the debate.

Term of office supplies one such safeguard. Short terms ensure that representatives ask again and often for the suffrages of their constituents. Frequent elections can thus protect against corruption at the top—provided, of course, that the electorate is not itself corrupt (preferring immediate, selfish interests ahead of enduring common goods); and frequent elections can bring forth new representatives replacing the old—provided that the electorate is not so sleepy and habit bound as to return officials irrespective of performance. On the other hand, short terms can leave the lawmaking body with little experience and little independence.

Concern that the electorate may indeed be this sleepy and habit bound is one reason for obliging them to try new people—otherwise even a short term of office might become in effect a lifetime appointment. **Rotation** is how this turnover is accomplished, and the Articles of Confederation provides the model, prescribing one-year terms for Congress members and permitting only three consecutive terms before requiring a time away of equal duration. Rotation is also desirable because it breaks apart cabals that form easily in legislative assemblies, and it forces politicians to experience as citizens the laws they created as lawmakers. But denying the electorate the right to elect the candidates of their choosing is undemocratic, say the other side. What's more, a career in office brings a touch of professionalism to a form of government noted for its amateurism.

Recall is a third safeguard. This failsafe device imposes instant punishment on wayward officials and prevents future harm done by them. Likely the recall is initiated by the state legislature, and either a new election is called in which the incumbent has to win the office a second time, or the state legislature, acting as the electorate, chooses a replacement. Recall can apply to both houses, upper and lower, but it makes better sense when applied to the upper house, or Senate, whose lengthy term of office—six years under the new Constitution—prevents timely correction by the represented party. The drawback is that recall mostly vitiates independence, which alarms some and gratifies others.

A kindred, but less fearsome instrument for controlling elected officials is **instructed voting**. Under this constraint the representative truly does represent another and not himself. But this represented party—the state legislature most likely—is not present to hear debate, and the instructed representative—a senator most likely—is not free to deliberate and compromise. The representative's job is rather to cast and defend a predetermined vote in a legislative chamber that makes little pretense to functioning as a deliberative body. Even so, dependency can be mitigated if instruction is advisory and not compulsory.

The Grand Federal Procession The engraving, by an unknown artist, shows the *Hamilton*, a miniature frigate turned into a float, drawn through the streets of New York City as part of a day-long parade called the Grand Federal Procession, held on July 23, 1788, in anticipation of New York's ratification. The float was used once before, on June 24, to celebrate the news that New Hampshire had ratified the Constitution.

Philip Van Cortlandt · Cornelius Schoonmaker · Peter Vrooman · John Haring · Israel Thompson · Robert R. Livingston · Melancton Smith · Governor George Clinton · Alexander Hamilton · Abraham Bancker · John Jay · James Clinton · Isaac Roosevelt · John Sloss Hobart · Jacobus Swartwout · Peter Vandervoort · James Duane · Philip Livingston · John Lansing · Lewis Morris · Richard Morris · Dirck Wyncoop · Gozen Ryerss

New York Ratifies! Pictured near the center are Governor Clinton and Alexander Hamilton shaking hands after the New York convention ratified the Constitution. The mural was painted by Gerald Foster in 1938 to commemorate the sesquicentennial of the event. It hangs in the Poughkeepsie post office.

Game Structure and Rules

Role-Play

Though mentioned already, it bears repeating that you are about to engage in role-play. You are entering a world not quite like your own. A leap of imagination is thus required, transporting you to the late eighteenth century, to a courthouse in Poughkeepsie, New York, there to debate the ratification of the Constitution. Game materials will help with the transition, but it is up to you to play the part.

The environment is a competitive one, with winners and losers, but also a collaborative one, with allies identified and neutrals to be courted. The better you know the history and writings of the period, the better your performance will be and, just possibly, the better the result. Study pays off.

But the exercise is called a game, because it is meant to be fun. And fun it is!

Convention Chair

Before the start of the game, the instructor will choose one student to serve as chair. The chair is an impartial, nonvoting moderator whose job is to introduce speakers and topics, enforce time limits at the podium, entertain comments from the floor, call for and keep tallies of the votes, and ensure that the convention completes its work on time. If historical names are adopted, the chair will be called Henry Oothoudt [OAT-howt], delegate from Albany and chair of the convention as it sat as a committee of the whole (a parliamentary device designed to facilitate free-wheeling debate). The game convention will sit only as a committee of the whole.

Factions

Each group of students is called a faction, or a party (these terms are used interchangeably). Faction members share the same group identity and the same victory objectives. Information about the political convictions of the faction and about game issues, bibliographical sources, and writing assignments can be found in the faction role sheet, which the instructor will provide. The distribution of faction roles is by lot, by choice of the students, or by choice of the instructor.

If class size allows, seven students are designated Federalists, seven as Antifederalists, and the remainder as Moderates.

The game also provides thirty-five individual delegate roles (with names, character biographies, and some game-play advice), which the instructor may wish to employ and may distribute deliberately or randomly. They are optional.

While public speaking is normally a part of role-play, limited time precludes formal speeches given by every delegate. Thus Federalist and Antifederalist delegates deliver speeches at the podium; Moderates act as judges and are the audience mainly addressed. In place of writing papers (the bases of speeches), Moderates take an exam to prepare for the game. As an inducement to do well, the student(s) scoring the highest grade casts an extra vote throughout the proceedings. The instructor may wish to count the exam grade as part of the course grade.

Leaders, Lieutenants, and Liaisons

Federalist and Antifederalist factions each choose (or the instructor chooses) a leader and a lieutenant. Their function is to divvy up work assignments, schedule and oversee strategy sessions, and generally ensure that the faction as a group is ready to make the most convincing case possible. If historical names are in use, the Federalist leader is Chancellor Robert R. Livingston, and the Federalist lieutenant is Alexander Hamilton; the Antifederalist leader is Governor George Clinton, and the Antifederalist lieutenant is Melancton Smith.

Moderates choose (or the instructor chooses) two, opposing organizers, who try moving Moderates toward the Federalists or toward the Antifederalists and who work as liaisons with the respective factions. Again, if historical names are in use, the Federalist liaison is Jonathan N. Havens, and the Antifederalist liaison is Jacobus Swartwout.

Vote Distributions

Voting occurs following debate on each of the game's seven issues (excluding the first), with a separate, and final, vote taken to determine acceptance or rejection of the Constitution. Every player casts one vote, except for the leader and the lieutenant of the Antifederalist faction, who each have two votes to start, a bonus meant to reflect the fact that, historically, the Antifederalists held a sizable majority at the New York State Ratifying Convention. But if New Hampshire ratifies while the New York convention is in session, the lieutenant's extra vote is eliminated. And if Virginia follows suit, the leader's extra vote is eliminated too. Die rolls will determine what transpires in these other states, with the odds set at 5-in-6 that New Hampshire ratifies and at 4-in-6 that Virginia ratifies. In the event of a vote to reject in New Hampshire (thus saving the lieutenant's extra vote), a vote to ratify in Virginia eliminates both the lieutenant's and the leader's extra vote.

Moderates, if called on by the chair to speak in debate, cast an extra vote on the provision to which they speak. The instructor will keep track, but it is each student's responsibility to invoke the privilege and cast the extra vote. The Moderate liaison whose faction has achieved a favorably rated Constitution after six provision votes casts an extra vote during the final vote. (On the rating of the Constitution by the instructor, see the next page.)

While one delegate–one vote is ordinarily the rule, extra votes are then cast by the Moderate exam winner(s) (throughout the game), by Moderate speakers (on provisions spoken to), by the Moderate liaison to the "provisionally" successful faction (during the final vote), and by the leader and lieutenant of the Antifederalist faction (unless and until New Hampshire and Virginia ratify).

Speeches, Debate, and Provision Votes

The expected procedure, provision by provision and through all game sessions, is as follows:

- Introductory remarks by the chair.

- Alternating speeches by Federalists and Antifederalists.

- Open-floor debate, including comments by Moderates.

- Caucusing (if needed and at the chair's discretion).

- Voting.

No voting is required during the first phase, which lays out competing theories of representation. During the second and third phases, votes occur following debate on each provision (unless, in the chair's or instructor's judgment, it is best to delay voting until debate is completed on related issues). Voting is by raised hand, to hurry the process along.

Rating the Constitution and Voting to Ratify

Each provision carries its own point total, information the instructor will provide before the final vote. A majority of points determines whether the package of provisions is classified as Federalist or Antifederalist. A vote cast for a package classified as Federalist is tantamount to a vote to ratify; a vote cast against such a package is tantamount to a vote to reject. Conversely, a vote for a package labeled Antifederalist is equivalent to a vote to reject, while a vote against such a package is equivalent to a vote to ratify.

In all cases, votes for and votes against represent acceptance or rejection of the Constitution's original design (given next, and in the appendix), not acceptance or rejection of the package of provisions produced in convention.

Constitution's Design (Article I.2.2; I.3.1; I.4.1)

The Constitution's several provisions affecting congressional representation are overwhelmingly Federalist. The size of the lower house, at least initially, is quite small—a mere sixty-five (no bigger than New York's house for a population ten times as large). And the size of the chamber determines inversely the size of electoral districts, which must be correspondingly large, albeit drawn by state legislatures. Terms are fixed for lower and upper houses and are indefinitely renewable—thus no recall or rotation. And instructed voting is not mandated or even mentioned—thus representatives and senators are free to exercise their own independent judgments.

On the other hand, the lower-house term of office—two years—is a compromise between the Antifederalist one year (as proposed in the Convention) and the Federalist three years (as proposed and initially passed in the Convention). The upper-house term of six years is longer than in any state (one year in most others and four years in New York), though shorter than the seven years provisionally approved, the nine years widely supported, and the lifetime appointments recommended by at least three Convention delegates.

In sum, of the six elements structuring congressional representation, five are fully Federalist and one is a blend.

Despite appearances to the contrary, the New York State convention is not rewriting the Constitution but approving or disapproving a draft of the Constitution written by others. Many of you will undoubtedly vote for provisions contrary to those contained in the Constitution, and you will likely behave in debate as if the Constitution were yours to compose. But it is not—acceptance or rejection is the issue.

This behavior was true, by the way, of the Antifederalists in Poughkeepsie, whom the Federalists allowed to propose amendments—in contravention of instructions from Philadelphia to give "assent and ratification"—as the price for proceeding slowly through the Constitution. Eventually, the Antifederalists came to realize that they were not amending exactly, but were making the case for rejection, for a new constitution, to be produced in a new convention. For their part, the Federalists in Poughkeepsie knew from the start that they were making the case for why the Constitution was sufficient as is, while allowing for the possibility of amendments in the future.

Much the same will be your experience here, in the game convention. It may therefore be helpful to think of provision votes on the size of the lower house, terms of office, rotation, recall, etc., as opinion polls forecasting the results of an election, which in the game is represented by the final vote.

Secession Option

If the final package is labeled Antifederalist, the leader of the Federalist faction, Chancellor Robert Livingston (if names are in use), may elect to exercise the secession option, i.e., to threaten the secession of the southern counties—New York, Richmond, Kings, and Westchester—from the rest of the state. The consequences of such a maneuver are hard to predict.

Second-Convention Option

Likewise, if the final package is labeled Federalist, the leader of the Antifederalist faction, Governor George Clinton (if names are in use), may elect to exercise the second-convention option, i.e., to threaten agitation on behalf of a second constitutional convention called to consider amendments arising from the various state conventions, with a **circular letter** as the main instrument of agitation. Again, the consequences are hard to predict.

> A **circular letter** was a document meant to circulate among official bodies or the general public. Papal letters to bishops, called encyclicals (Greek for "in a circle"), were the prototype of circular letters.

Final Vote

The final vote, although on the representation issue only, serves as a surrogate for the convention's decision to ratify or reject the Constitution. Once the package is scored Federalist or Antifederalist, no debate is to occur, just the final vote.

A tie vote here occasions, in the first instance, a do-over vote, which, if still a tie, is resolved in the second instance by a die roll, with the odds set at

50–50. (If a tie meant rejection, as is normally the case, then the opposition would have an advantage—winning any tie—and it would be in the interest of the parties, quite perversely, for the package of provisions to be rated against them by the instructor.)

The convention chair, ordinarily a nonvoting member, does vote on the final package.

Voting here is one by one, if time permits and the number of players is not too large. The game ends with this vote.

Game Schedules

Two schedules are provided here, one for courses meeting twice a week, the other for courses meeting three times a week. If weekly class sessions exceed, or fall short of, 150 minutes, the instructor will make adjustments

GAME SCHEDULE 1

Two Weekly Class Meetings (75 minutes each)

CLASS SESSIONS	DEBATE PHASES	CONSTITUTIONAL ISSUES AND PROVISIONS	Classifications/Objectives	
			FEDERALIST	ANTIFEDERALIST
1	First Phase	1. Character of Representative	trustee	agent
	Second Phase	2. Size of Chamber	1 per 30,000 large	1 per 20,000 small
		3. Size of Electoral Districts		
2	Third Phase	4. Term of Office (House)	2 years	1 year
		Term of Office (Senate)	6 years	3 years
		5. Rotation	no	yes
		6. Recall	no	yes
		7. Instructed Voting	no	yes
	Final Vote			
	Debriefing			

Three Weekly Class Meetings (50 minutes each)

CLASS SESSIONS	DEBATE PHASES	CONSTITUTIONAL ISSUES AND PROVISIONS	Classifications/Objectives	
			FEDERALIST	ANTIFEDERALIST
1	First Phase	1. Character of Representative	trustee	agent
	Second Phase	2. Size of Chamber	1 per 30,000	1 per 20,000
2	Second Phase	3. Size of Electoral Districts	large	small
	Third Phase	4. Term of Office (House)	2 years	1 year
		Term of Office (Senate)	6 years	3 years
		5. Rotation	no	yes
3	Third Phase	6. Recall	no	yes
		7. Instructed Voting	no	yes
	Final Vote			
	Debriefing			

(e.g., more speeches, added time for setup and debriefing, in the former; consolidation of issues, in the latter). The game classifies particular positions or outcomes as Federalist or Antifederalist; these classifications also represent faction objectives; they thus are listed under "Classifications/Objectives."

Contemporary Resonances

As hinted at in the introduction to the game book, Federalist and Antifederalist positions on the qualities and responsibilities of elected officials are very much with us today. Following are some examples.

A challenge put to candidates to give evidence of readiness for office (whether previous offices held or payrolls met or service in the military) is Federalist in origin; whereas a demand to disclose tax returns or reveal details of private life is Antifederalist. The first speaks to competence, the second speaks to character: Are you capable? Are you trustworthy?

Claims of "outsider" status by one candidate or the other—and not infrequently by both—are Antifederalist in kind, since they tap into the public's anxiety about the corrupting effects of office and power, while offering assurances of innocence and honesty based on distance from and unfamiliarity with the sordid ways of Washington—aka the "swamp." Conversely, confident promises to "bring home the bacon" and proud tallies of federal dollars already procured are Federalist in kind, since they stand as proof that representatives know how to work the system for the benefit of their constituents.

Autobiographies showing humble beginnings and "I feel your pain" professions of empathy are Antifederalist, as these establish kinship with the people; no less Antifederalist is the animus felt toward, or the suspicions directed against, the wealthy and the Ivy League educated. On the other side, it is Federalist to boast of the endorsements of party officials and editorial boards and to advertise advanced degrees earned.

Is a politician to be castigated for "flip-flopping" on the issues, for finger-in-the-wind position taking? The accusation of flip-flopping is Federalist: lack of core character, an independent mind, or the courage of one's convictions. The practice of flip-flopping, however, is Antifederalist: faithful representation of the inconstant desires of the public.

Although believing themselves at opposite ends of the ideological spectrum, Tea Party types and Occupy Wall Street types are both Antifederalist, the one decrying the waste, fraud, and abuse of big government, the other railing against the greed and corruption of big business. Bigness is bad, they avow; it breeds arrogance, operates in secret, serves selfish purposes, and crushes the weak and the voiceless—all Antifederalist sentiments. But candidates who bankroll their own campaigns and sing of their success are Federalist in spirit, their message being—I have made it, and, if elected, I will help you make it too.

A policy issue closely related to electoral politics is campaign finance reform. Those citizen groups earnestly determined to stanch the flow of money into politics are the intellectual heirs of Antifederalism, which cried "aristocracy" whenever it seemed that the elites were taking advantage. Money buys influence, privileging the few over the many. Federalism has no convincing retort to this populist complaint, at least none that it dares utter publicly at election time. Federalism instead shows in the actions that candidates take: they all raise money, gobs of it, priding themselves on having raised more than their opponents, even while denouncing the corruption and impugning the legitimacy of big-money contributions.

Another policy debate currently dividing Washington is the growing power of the administrative state. Should lawmaking be the preserve of the legislative branch (as per Article I of the Constitution: "all legislative powers herein granted shall be vested in a Congress of the United States"), whose officeholders are elected by and answerable to the people, or should experts in the bureaucracy, permanent employees beyond the reach of popular control, in effect make laws (though called regulations), following vague and aspirational guidelines set by Congress? Those inclining toward the former view are of the Antifederalist persuasion, those toward the latter of the Federalist persuasion.

If it seems difficult to draw straight lines connecting Federalist and Antifederalist attitudes to the political parties today, the reason may be that both parties, Democratic and Republican, seek support from an electorate that has never quite decided what a representative should be and do. And so the debate begun in the Founding period continues to this day.

Part 4

Core Texts

EDMUND BURKE

FROM Speech to the Electors of Bristol, 1774

Edmund Burke (1729–1797) was a noted political theorist and long-serving member of Parliament during the latter half of the eighteenth century. He represented the town of Bristol from 1774 to 1780. On November 3, 1774, he delivered a campaign speech to the 5,000 electors of Bristol, explaining his understanding of the duties of an elected official. These duties went beyond—or fell short of—exact representation of the views and interests of his constituents.

Source: *The Works of the Right Honourable Edmund Burke,* vol. 1 (London: Henry G. Bohn, 1854), pp. 446–48.

THOUGHT QUESTION: If you would not want your neighbors performing surgery on your heart or installing the plumbing in your house, why do you want their ill-considered opinions reflected in the laws you have to obey?

Certainly, gentlemen, it ought to be the happiness and glory of a representative to live in the strictest union, the closest correspondence, and the most unreserved communication with his constituents. Their wishes ought to have great weight with him; their opinion, high respect; their business, unremitted attention. It is his duty to sacrifice his repose, his pleasures, his satisfactions, to theirs; and above all, ever, and in all cases, to prefer their interest to his own. But his unbiassed opinion, his mature judgment, his enlightened conscience, he ought not to sacrifice to you, to any man, or to any set of men living. These he does not derive from your pleasure; no, nor from the law and the constitution. They are a trust from Providence, for the abuse of which he is deeply answerable. Your representative owes you, not his industry only, but his judgment; and he betrays, instead of serving you, if he sacrifices it to your opinion.

My worthy colleague says, his will ought to be subservient to yours. If that be all, the thing is innocent. If government were a matter of will upon any side, yours, without question, ought to be superior. But government and legislation are matters of reason and judgment, and not of inclination; and what sort of reason is that, in which the determination precedes the discussion; in which one set of men deliberate, and another decide; and where those who form the conclusion are perhaps three hundred miles distant from those who hear the arguments?

To deliver an opinion, is the right of all men; that of constituents is a weighty and respectable opinion, which a representative ought always to rejoice to hear; and which he ought always most seriously to consider. But *authoritative* instructions; *mandates* issued, which the member is bound blindly and implicitly to obey, to vote, and to argue for, though contrary to the clearest conviction of his judgment and conscience—these are things utterly unknown to the laws of this land, and which arise from a fundamental mistake of the whole order and tenor of our constitution.

An ambassador communicates opinions and casts votes for an authority not present. A representative deliberates with others and exercises his or her own independent judgment. But does this understanding of representation apply only in homogenous societies with interests common to all?

Parliament is not a *congress* of ambassadors from different and hostile interests; which interests each must maintain, as an agent and advocate, against other agents and advocates; but parliament is a *deliberative* assembly of *one* nation, with *one* interest, that of the whole; where, not local purposes, not local prejudices, ought to guide, but the general good, resulting from the general reason of the whole. You choose a member indeed; but when you have chosen him, he is not a member of Bristol, but he is a member of *parliament*. If the local constituent should have an interest, or should form an hasty opinion, evidently opposite to the real good of the rest of the community, the member for that place ought to be as far, as any other, from any endeavour to give it effect.

PUBLIUS

FROM *The Federalist*, 1787–88

"Publius" was the pseudonym for Alexander Hamilton, John Jay, and James Madison, who together authored the eighty-five essays included in The Federalist. *Published serially in the* Independent Journal, *the* New York Packet, *and the* Daily Advertiser *between October 1787 and April 1788, the essays were collected in a two-volume book brought out by J. & A. Mclean in March and May, 1788 under the title* The Federalist: A Collection of Essays, Written in Favour of the New Constitution, as Agreed upon by the Federal Convention, September 17, 1787. *The selections reprinted here give the Federalist view of congressional representation.*

Source: Alexander Hamilton, John Jay, and James Madison, *The Federalist* (Philadelphia: R. Wilson Desilver, 1847), pp. 36–37, 130–33, 229–37.

THOUGHT QUESTION: How much trust should be placed in the people operating as the electorate?

JAMES MADISON, FROM *FEDERALIST* 10

. . . A republic, by which I mean a government in which the scheme of representation takes place, opens a different prospect, and promises the cure [for faction][1] for which we are seeking. Let us examine the points in which it varies from pure democracy, and we shall comprehend both the nature of the cure and the efficacy which it must derive from the union.

The two great points of difference between a democracy and a republic are: first, the delegation of the government, in the latter, to a small number of citizens elected by the rest; secondly, the greater number of citizens, and greater sphere of country, over which the latter may be extended.

The effect of the first difference is, on the one hand, to refine and enlarge the public views, by passing them through the medium of a chosen body of citizens, whose wisdom may best discern the true interest of their country, and whose patriotism and love of justice will be least likely to sacrifice it to temporary or partial considerations. Under such a regulation, it may well happen that the public voice, pronounced by the representatives of the people, will be more consonant to the public good than if pronounced by the people themselves, convened for the purpose. On the other hand, the effect may be inverted. Men of factious tempers, of local prejudices, or of sinister designs, may, by intrigue, by corruption, or by other means, first obtain the suffrages, and then betray the interests, of the people. The question resulting is, whether small or extensive republics are more favorable to the election of proper guardians of the public weal [common good]; and it is clearly decided in favor of the latter by two obvious considerations:

In the first place, it is to be remarked that, however small the republic may be, the representatives must be raised to a certain number, in order to guard against the cabals of a few; and that, however large it may be, they must be limited to a certain number, in order to guard against the confusion of a multitude. Hence, the number of representatives in the two cases not

> Representatives should refine public opinion, not simply reflect it. Large republics are more likely to have such "fit characters" to choose from, and large electorates are more likely to prefer them.

---

1. Elsewhere in *Federalist* 10, Madison defines faction as "a number of citizens, whether amounting to a majority or minority of the whole, who are united and actuated by some common impulse of passion, or of interest, adverse to the rights of other citizens, or to the permanent and aggregate interests of the community."

being in proportion to that of the two constituents, and being proportionally greater in the small republic, it follows that, if the proportion of fit characters be not less in the large than in the small republic, the former will present a greater option, and consequently a greater probability of a fit choice.

In the next place, as each representative will be chosen by a greater number of citizens in the large than in the small republic, it will be more difficult for unworthy candidates to practice with success the vicious arts by which elections are too often carried; and the suffrages of the people being more free, will be more likely to center in men who possess the most attractive merit and the most diffusive and established characters.

It must be confessed that in this, as in most other cases, there is a mean, on both sides of which inconveniences will be found to lie. By enlarging too much the number of electors, you render the representatives too little acquainted with all their local circumstances and lesser interests; as by reducing it too much, you render him unduly attached to these, and too little fit to comprehend and pursue great and national objects. The federal constitution forms a happy combination in this respect; the great and aggregate interests being referred to the national, the local and particular to the state legislatures. . . .

ALEXANDER HAMILTON, FROM *FEDERALIST* 35

. . . One [objection] which, if we may judge from the frequency of its repetition, seems most to be relied on, is, that the house of representatives is not sufficiently numerous for the reception of all the different classes of citizens, in order to combine the interests and feelings of every part of the community, and to produce a due sympathy between the representative body and its constituents. This argument presents itself under a very specious and seducing form; and is well calculated to lay hold of the prejudices of those to whom it is addressed. But when we come to dissect it with attention, it will appear to be made up of nothing but fair-sounding words. The object it seems to aim at is, in the first place, impracticable, and in the sense in which it is contended for, is unnecessary. I reserve for another place the discussion of the question which relates to the sufficiency of the representative body in respect to numbers, and shall content myself with examining here the particular use which has been made of a contrary supposition, in reference to the immediate subject of our inquiries.

The idea of an actual representation of all classes of the people, by persons of each class, is altogether visionary. Unless it were expressly provided in the Constitution that each different occupation should send one or more members, the thing would never take place in practice. Mechanics and manufacturers will always be inclined, with few exceptions, to give their votes to merchants, in preference to persons of their own professions or trades.

Those discerning citizens are well aware that the mechanic and manufacturing arts furnish the materials of mercantile enterprise and industry. Many of them, indeed, are immediately connected with the operations of commerce. They know that the merchant is their natural patron and friend; and they are aware, that however great the confidence they may justly feel in their own good sense, their interests can be more effectually promoted by the merchant than by themselves. They are sensible that their habits in life have not been such as to give them those acquired endowments, without which, in a deliberative assembly, the greatest natural abilities are for the most part useless; and that the influence and weight, and superior acquirements of the merchants render them more equal to a contest with any spirit which might happen to infuse itself into the public councils, unfriendly to the manufacturing and trading interests. These considerations, and many others that might be mentioned prove, and experience confirms it, that artisans and manufacturers will commonly be disposed to bestow their votes upon merchants and those whom they recommend. We must therefore consider merchants as the natural representatives of all these classes of the community.

With regard to the learned professions,[2] little need be observed; they truly form no distinct interest in society, and according to their situation and talents, will be indiscriminately the objects of the confidence and choice of each other, and of other parts of the community.

Nothing remains but the landed interest; and this, in a political view, and particularly in relation to taxes, I take to be perfectly united, from the wealthiest landlord down to the poorest tenant. No tax can be laid on land which will not affect the proprietor of millions of acres as well as the proprietor of a single acre. Every landholder will therefore have a common interest to keep the taxes on land as low as possible; and common interest may always be reckoned upon as the surest bond of sympathy. But if we even could suppose a distinction of

---

2. Lawyers are mainly intended, but also physicians, academics, and ministers.

interest between the opulent landholder and the middling farmer, what reason is there to conclude, that the first would stand a better chance of being deputed to the national legislature than the last? If we take fact as our guide, and look into our own senate and assembly, we shall find that moderate proprietors of land prevail in both; nor is this less the case in the senate, which consists of a smaller number, than in the assembly, which is composed of a greater number. Where the qualifications of the electors are the same, whether they have to choose a small or a large number, their votes will fall upon those in whom they have most confidence; whether these happen to be men of large fortunes, or of moderate property, or of no property at all.

It is said to be necessary, that all classes of citizens should have some of their own number in the representative body, in order that their feelings and interests may be the better understood and attended to. But we have seen that this will never happen under any arrangement that leaves the votes of the people free. Where this is the case, the representative body, with too few exceptions to have any influence on the spirit of the government, will be composed of landholders, merchants, and men of the learned professions. But where is the danger that the interests and feelings of the different classes of citizens will not be understood or attended to by these three descriptions of men? Will not the landholder know and feel whatever will promote or insure the interest of landed property? And will he not, from his own interest in that species of property, be sufficiently prone to resist every attempt to prejudice or encumber it? Will not the merchant understand and be disposed to cultivate, as far as may be proper, the interests of the mechanic and manufacturing arts, to which his commerce is so nearly allied? Will not the man of the learned profession, who will feel a neutrality to the rivalships between the different branches of industry, be likely to prove an impartial arbiter between them, ready to promote either, so far as it shall appear to him conducive to the general interests of the community?

If we take into the account the momentary humors or dispositions which may happen to prevail in particular parts of the society, and to which a wise administration will never be inattentive, is the man whose situation leads to extensive inquiry and information less likely to be a competent judge of their nature, extent, and foundation than one whose observation does not travel beyond the circle of his neighbors and acquaintances? Is it not natural that a man who is a candidate for the favor of the people, and who is dependent on the suffrages of his fellow-citizens for the continuance of his public honors, should take care to inform himself of their dispositions and inclinations, and should be willing to allow them their proper degree of influence upon his conduct? This dependence, and the necessity of being bound himself, and his posterity, by the laws to which he gives his assent, are the true, and they are the strong chords of sympathy between the representative and the constituent.

There is no part of the administration of government that requires extensive information and a thorough knowledge of the principles of political economy, so much as the business of taxation. The man who understands those principles best will be least likely to resort to oppressive expedients, or sacrifice any particular class of citizens to the procurement of revenue. It might be demonstrated that the most productive system of finance will always be the least burdensome. There can be no doubt that in order to a judicious exercise of the power of taxation, it is necessary that the person in whose hands it should be acquainted with the general genius, habits, and modes of thinking of the people at large, and with the resources of the country. And this is all that can be reasonably meant by a knowledge of the interests and feelings of the people. In any other sense the proposition has either no meaning, or an absurd one. And in that sense let every considerate citizen judge for himself where the requisite qualification is most likely to be found.

JAMES MADISON, FROM *FEDERALIST* 57

The *third* charge against the house of representatives is, that it will be taken from that class of citizens which will have least sympathy with the mass of the people, and be most likely to aim at an ambitious sacrifice of the many to the aggrandizement of the few.

Of all the objections which have been framed against the federal constitution, this is perhaps the most extraordinary. Whilst the objection itself is levelled against a pretended oligarchy, the principle of it strikes at the very root of republican government.

The aim of every political constitution is, or ought to be, first to obtain for rulers men who possess most wisdom to discern, and most virtue to pursue, the common good of the society; and in the next place, to take the most effectual precautions for keeping them virtuous whilst they continue to hold their public trust. The elective mode of obtaining rulers is the characteristic policy of republican government. The means relied on in this form of government for preventing their degeneracy are numerous and various. The most effectual one, is such a limitation of the term of appointments as will maintain a proper responsibility to the people.

Let me now ask what circumstance there is in the constitution of the house of representatives that violates the principles of republican government, or favors the elevation of the few on the ruins of the many? Let me ask whether every circumstance is not, on the contrary, strictly conformable to these principles, and scrupulously impartial to the rights and pretensions of every class and description of citizens?

Who are to be the electors of the federal representatives? Not the rich, more than the poor; not the learned, more than the ignorant; not the haughty heirs of distinguished names, more than the humble sons of obscurity and unpropitious fortune. The electors are to be the great body of the people of the United States. They are to be the same who exercise the right in every State of electing the corresponding branch of the legislature of the state.

Who are to be the objects of popular choice? Every citizen whose merit may recommend him to the esteem and confidence of his country. No qualification of wealth, of birth, of religious faith, or of civil profession is permitted to fetter the judgment or disappoint the inclination of the people.

If we consider the situation of the men on whom the free suffrages of their fellow-citizens may confer the representative trust, we shall find it involving every security which can be devised or desired for their fidelity to their constituents.

In the first place, as they will have been distinguished by the preference of their fellow-citizens, we are to presume that in general they will be somewhat distinguished also by those qualities which entitle them to it, and which promise a sincere and scrupulous regard to the nature of their engagements.

In the second place, they will enter into the public service under circumstances which cannot fail to produce a temporary affection at least to their constituents. There is in every breast a sensibility to marks of honor, of favor, of esteem, and of confidence, which, apart from all considerations of interest, is some pledge for grateful and benevolent returns. Ingratitude is a common topic of declamation against human nature; and it must be confessed that instances of it are but too frequent and flagrant, both in public and in private life. But the universal and extreme indignation which it inspires is itself a proof of the energy and prevalence of the contrary sentiment.

In the third place, those ties which bind the representative to his constituents are strengthened by motives of a more selfish nature. His pride and vanity attach him to a form of government which favors his pretensions and gives him a share in its honors and distinctions. Whatever hopes or projects might be entertained by a few aspiring characters, it must generally happen that a great proportion of the men deriving their advancement from their influence with the people, would have more to hope from a preservation of the favor, than from innovations in the government subversive of the authority of the people.

All these securities, however, would be found very insufficient without the restraint of frequent elections. Hence, in the fourth place, the house of representatives is so constituted as to support in the members an habitual recollection of their dependence on the people. Before the sentiments impressed on their minds by the mode of their elevation can be effaced by the exercise of power, they will be compelled to anticipate the moment when their power is to cease, when their exercise of it is to be reviewed, and when they must descend to the level from which they were raised; there forever to remain unless a faithful discharge of their trust shall have established their title to a renewal of it.

> Office separates its holder from the people served. But a short tenure reestablishes dependency and is a powerful reminder of who's in charge.

I will add, as a fifth circumstance in the situation of the house of representatives, restraining them from oppressive measures, that they can make no law which will not have its full operation on themselves and their friends, as well as on the great mass of the society. This has always been deemed one of the strongest bonds by which human policy can connect the rulers and the people together. It creates between them that communion of interests and sympathy of sentiments, of which few governments have furnished examples; but without which every government degenerates into tyranny. If it be asked, what is to restrain the House of Representatives from making legal discriminations in favor of themselves and a particular class of the society? I answer: the genius of the whole system; the nature of just and constitutional laws; and above all, the vigilant and manly spirit which actuates the people of America; a spirit which nourishes freedom, and in return is nourished by it.

If this spirit shall ever be so far debased as to tolerate a law not obligatory on the legislature, as well as on the people, the people will be prepared to tolerate anything but liberty.

Such will be the relation between the house of representatives and their constituents. Duty, gratitude, interest, ambition itself, are the chords by which they will be bound to fidelity and sympathy with the great mass of the people. It is possible that these may all be insufficient to control the caprice and wickedness of man. But are they not all that government will admit, and that human prudence can devise? Are they not the genuine and the characteristic means by which republican government provides for the liberty and happiness of the people? Are they not the identical means on which every State government in the union relies for the attainment of these important ends? What then are we to understand by the objection which this paper has combated? What are we to say to the men who profess the most flaming zeal for republican government, yet boldly impeach the fundamental principle of it; who pretend to be champions for the right and the capacity of the people to choose their own rulers, yet maintain that they will prefer those only who will immediately and infallibly betray the trust committed to them?

Were the objection to be read by one who had not seen the mode prescribed by the constitution for the choice of representatives, he could suppose nothing less than that some unreasonable qualification of property was annexed to the right of suffrage; or that the right of eligibility was limited to persons of particular families or fortunes; or at least that the mode prescribed by the State constitutions was in some respect or other, very grossly departed from. We have seen how far such a supposition would err, as to the two first points. Nor would it, in fact, be less erroneous as to the last. The only difference discoverable between the two cases is, that each representative of the United States will be elected by five or six thousand citizens; whilst in the individual States, the election of a representative is left to about as many hundreds. Will it be pretended that this difference is sufficient to justify an attachment to the State governments, and an abhorrence to the federal government? If this be the point on which the objection turns, it deserves to be examined.

Is it supported by *reason?* This cannot be said, without maintaining that five or six thousand citizens are less capable of choosing a fit representative, or more liable to be corrupted by an unfit one, than five or six hundred. Reason, on the contrary, assures us, that as in so great a number

> Sympathy born of similarity of circumstances (a point insisted on by Antifederalists) is not so important given other emotional ties binding representatives to constituents and given such structural checks as biennial elections.

a fit representative would be most likely to be found, so the choice would be less likely to be diverted from him by the intrigues of the ambitious or the bribes of the rich.

Is the *consequence* from this doctrine admissible? If we say that five or six hundred citizens are as many as can jointly exercise their right of suffrage, must we not deprive the people of the immediate choice of their public servants, in every instance where the administration of the government does not require as many of them as will amount to one for that number of citizens? . . .

JAMES MADISON, FROM *FEDERALIST* 58

. . . One observation however I must be permitted, to add, on this subject, as claiming, in my judgment, a very serious attention. It is, that in all legislative assemblies, the greater the number composing them may be, the fewer will be the men who will in fact direct their proceedings. In the first place, the more numerous any assembly may be, of whatever characters composed, the greater is known to be the ascendancy of passion over reason. In the next place, the larger the number, the greater will be the proportion of members of limited information and of weak capacities. Now it is precisely on characters of this description, that the eloquence and address of the few are known to act with all their force. In the ancient republics, where the whole body of the people assembled in person, a single orator, or an artful statesman, was generally seen to rule with as complete a sway, as if a sceptre had been placed in his single hands. On the same principle the more multitudinous a representative assembly may be rendered, the more it will partake of the infirmities incident to collective meetings of the people. Ignorance will be the dupe of cunning; and passion the slave of sophistry and declamation. The people can never err more than in supposing that by multiplying their representatives, beyond a certain limit, they strengthen the barrier against the government of a few. Experience will forever admonish them, that, on the contrary, *after securing a sufficient number for the purposes of safety, of local information, and of diffusive sympathy with the whole society,* they will counteract their own views by every addition to their representatives. The countenance of the government may become more democratic; but the soul that animates it will be more oligarchic. The machine will be enlarged, but the fewer and often, the more secret will be the springs by which its motions are directed. . . .

FEDERAL FARMER

FROM *Letters from the Federal Farmer*, 1787–88

It is not known for certain who authored the Letters from the Federal Farmer. *Richard Henry Lee of Virginia was long thought to be the author, mainly on the strength of an article published in the* Connecticut Courant *in December 1787 naming Lee as the author. But little else in Lee's writings or biography supports the attribution. More recent scholarship credits Melancton Smith of New York. The* Letters, *eighteen in total, came in two installments, printed in the Poughkeepsie* Country Journal *and in pamphlet form, and appearing between October 1787 and January 1788. The selections from letters 7, 8, and 9 detail the Antifederalist view of congressional representation.*

Source: Federal Farmer, *An Additional number of Letters from the Federal Farmer to the Republican; Leading to a Fair Examination of the System of Government, Proposed by the Late Convention; to Several Essential and Necessary Alterations to It; and Calculated to Illustrate and Support the Principles and Positions Laid Down in the Preceding Letters* (New York: Unspecified printer, 1788), pp. 56–63, 69–81 (with some spellings modernized, notes added, and minor alterations made).

THOUGHT QUESTION: Does "just like me" representation depend on the postulate that society is ineluctably divided into classes of few and many, rich and poor, strong and weak?

FROM *LETTER 7*

. . . It being impracticable for the people to assemble to make laws, they must elect legislators, and assign men to the different departments of the government. In the representative branch we must expect chiefly to collect the confidence of the people, and in it to find almost entirely the force of persuasion. In forming this branch, therefore, several important considerations must be attended to. It must possess abilities to discern the situation of the people and of public affairs, a disposition to sympathize with the people, and a capacity and inclination to make laws congenial to their circumstances and condition: it must afford security against interested combinations, corruption and influence; it must possess the confidence, and have the voluntary support of the people.

I think these positions will not be controverted, nor the one I formerly advanced, that a fair and equal representation is that in which the interests, feelings, opinions and views of the people are collected, in such manner as they would be were the people all assembled. Having made these general observations, I shall proceed to consider further my principal position, viz. that there is no substantial representation of the people provided for in a government, in which the most essential powers, even as to the internal police of the country, are proposed to be lodged; and to propose certain amendments as to the representative branch: 1st, That there ought to be *an increase of the numbers of representatives:* And, 2dly. That the elections of them ought to be better secured.

The representation is unsubstantial and ought to be increased. In matters where there is much room for opinion, you will not expect me to establish my positions with mathematical certainty; you must only expect my observations to be candid, and such as are well founded in the mind of the writer. I am in a field where doctors disagree; and as to genuine representation, though no feature in government can be more important, perhaps, no one has been less understood, and no one that has received so imperfect a consideration by political writers. The ephori in Sparta, and the tribunes in Rome, were but the shadow; the representation in Great-Britain is unequal and insecure.[1] In America we have done more in establishing this important branch on its true principles, than, perhaps, all the world besides: yet even here, I conceive, that very great improvements in representation may be made.

In fixing this branch, the situation of the people must be surveyed, and the number of representatives and forms of election apportioned to that situation. When we find a numerous people settled in a fertile and extensive country, possessing equality, and few or none of them oppressed with riches or wants, it ought to be the anxious care of the constitution and laws, to arrest them from national depravity, and to preserve them in their happy condition. A virtuous people make just laws, and good laws tend to preserve unchanged a virtuous people. A virtuous and happy people by laws uncongenial to their characters, may easily be gradually changed into servile and depraved creatures. Where the people, or their representatives, make the laws, it is probable they will generally be fitted to the national character and circumstances, unless the representation be partial, and the imperfect substitute of the people. However, the people may be electors, [but] if the representation be so formed as to give

---

1. Sparta's five ephors (overseers) were elected annually by the assembly; they were more magistrates than representatives, however, running the state when the kings were away at war. Rome's tribunes, two at first rising to ten, represented the people judicially; but as their powers expanded into other areas, their popular purpose waned. British representation in the House of Commons was notoriously uneven, with some pastures having more representation than some cities.

one or more of the natural classes of men in the society an undue ascendency over the others, it is imperfect; the former will gradually become masters, and the latter slaves. It is the first of all among the political balances, to preserve in its proper station each of these classes. We talk of balances in the legislature, and among the departments of government; we ought to carry them to the body of the people.

Balancing the classes of society is just as important as balancing the branches of government.

Since I advanced the idea of balancing the several orders of men in a community, in forming a genuine representation, and seen that idea considered as chimerical.[2] I have been sensibly struck with a sentence in the marquis Beccaria's treatise: this sentence was quoted by congress in 1774, and is as follows: "In every society there is an effort continually tending to confer on one part the height of power and happiness, and to reduce the others to the extreme of weakness and misery; the intent of good laws is to oppose this effort, and to diffuse their influence universally and equally."[3] Add to this Montesquieu's opinion, that "in a free state every man, who is supposed to be a free agent, ought to be concerned in his own government: therefore, the legislative should reside in the whole body of the people, or their representatives."[4] It is extremely clear that these writers had in view the several orders of men in society, which we call aristocratical, democratical, merchantile, mechanic, &c. and perceived the efforts they are constantly, from interested and ambitious views, disposed to make to elevate themselves and oppress others. Each order must have a share in the business of legislation actually and efficiently. It is deceiving a people to tell them they are electors, and can chuse their legislators, if they cannot, in the nature of things, chuse men from among themselves, and genuinely like themselves.

I wish you to take another idea along with you; we are not only to balance these natural efforts, but we are also to guard against accidental combinations; combinations founded in the connections of offices and private interests, both evils which are increased in proportion as the number of men, among which the elected must be, are decreased.

---

2. "Chimerical" is derived from chimera, a mythical monster compounded of a lion's head, a goat's body, and a serpent's tail. The word denotes a fantasy or mental illusion.

3. Cesare Bonesana Beccaria, *An Essay on Crimes and Punishments*, Introduction.

4. Charles Louis de Secondat, Baron de Montesquieu, *The Spirit of the Laws*, XI.6. With this quotation (and its following sentence), Montesquieu sets up the Antifederalist position that representation is a necessity of size properly constituted when the representative is a replica of the represented.

To set this matter in a proper point of view, we must form some general ideas and descriptions of the different classes of men, as they may be divided by occupations and politically: the first class is the aristocratical. There are three kinds of aristocracy spoken of in this country—the first is a constitutional one, which does not exist in the United States in our common acceptation of the word. Montesquieu, it is true, observes, that where a part of the persons in a society, for want of property, age, or moral character, are excluded any share in the government, the others, who alone are the constitutional electors and elected, form this aristocracy [II.2]; this, according to him, exists in each of the United States, where a considerable number of persons, as all convicted of crimes, under age, or not possessed of certain property, are excluded any share in the government;—the second is an aristocratic faction; a junto of unprincipled men, often distinguished for their wealth or abilities, who combine together and make their object their private interests and aggrandizement; the existence of this description is merely accidental, but particularly to be guarded against. The third is the natural aristocracy; this term we use to designate a respectable order of men, the line between whom and the natural democracy is in some degree arbitrary; we may place men on one side of this line, which others may place on the other, and in all disputes between the few and the many, a considerable number are wavering and uncertain themselves on which side they are, or ought to be.

In my idea of our natural aristocracy in the United States, I include about four or five thousand men; and among these I reckon those who have been placed in the offices of governors, of members of Congress, and state senators generally, in the principal officers of Congress, of the army and militia, the superior judges, the most eminent professional men, &c. and men of large property—the other persons and orders in the community form the natural democracy; this includes in general the yeomanry, the subordinate officers, civil and military, the fishermen, mechanics and traders, many of the merchants and professional men.

It is easy to perceive that men of these two classes, the aristocratical, and democratical, with views equally honest, have sentiments widely different, especially respecting public and private expences, salaries, taxes, &c. Men of the first class associate more extensively, have a high sense of honor, possess abilities, ambition, and general knowledge; men of the second class are not so much used to combining great objects; they possess less ambition, and a larger share of honesty: their dependence is principally on middling and small estates, industrious pursuits, and hard labour, while that of the former is principally on the emoluments of large estates, and of the chief offices of government.

> Society's main factional divide is between the natural aristocracy, distinguished by its ability, and the natural democracy, distinguished by its honesty. Each class though is alike in wanting to shift its expenses onto the other.

Not only the efforts of these two great parties are to be balanced, but other interests and parties also, which do not always oppress each other merely for want of power, and for fear of the consequences; though they, in fact, mutually depend on each other; yet such are their general views, that the merchants alone would never fail to make laws favourable to themselves and oppressive to the farmers, &c. the farmers alone would act on like principles; the former would tax the land, the latter the trade. The manufacturers are often disposed to contend for monopolies, buyers make every exertion to lower prices, and sellers to raise them; men who live by fees and salaries endeavour to raise them, and the part of the people who pay them, endeavour to lower them; the public creditors to augment the taxes, and the people at large to lessen them. Thus, in every period of society, and in all the transactions of men, we see parties verifying the observation made by the Marquis; and those classes which have not their centinels in the government, in proportion to what they have to gain or lose, most infallibly be ruined.

Efforts among parties are not merely confined to property; they contend for rank and distinctions; all their passions in turn are enlisted in political controversies—Men, elevated in society, are often disgusted with the changeableness of the democracy, and the latter are often agitated with the passions of jealousy and envy: the yeomanry possess a large share of property and strength, are nervous and firm in their opinions and habits—the mechanics of towns are ardent and changeable, honest and credulous, they are inconsiderable for numbers, weight and strength, not always sufficiently stable for the supporting free governments: the fishing interest partakes partly of the strength and stability of the landed, and partly of the changeableness of the mechanic interest. As to merchants and traders, they are our agents in almost all money transactions; give activity to government, and possess a considerable share of influence in it.

It has been observed by an able writer, that frugal industrious merchants are generally advocates for liberty. It is an observation, I believe, well founded, that the schools produce but few advocates for republican forms of government; gentlemen of the law, divinity, physic, &c. probably form about a fourth part of the people; yet their political influence, perhaps, is equal to that of all the other descriptions of men; if we may judge from the appointments to Congress, the legal characters will often, in a small representation, be the majority; but the more the representatives are encreased, the more of the farmers, merchants, &c. will be found to be brought into the government.

These general observations will enable you to discern what I intend by different classes, and the general scope of my ideas, when I contend for uniting and balancing their interests, feelings, opinions, and views in the legislature; we may not only so unite and balance these as to prevent a change in the government by the gradual exaltation of one part to the depression of others, but we may derive many other advantages from the combination and full representation; a small representation can never be well informed as to the circumstances of the people, the members of it must be too far removed from the people, in general, to sympathize with them, and too few to communicate with them: a representation must be extremely imperfect where the representatives are not circumstanced to make the proper communications to their constituents, and where the constituents in turn cannot, with tolerable convenience, make known their wants, circumstances, and opinions, to their representatives; where there is but one representative to 30,000 or 40,000 inhabitants, it appears to me, he can only mix, and be acquainted with a few respectable characters among his constituents, even double the federal representation, and then there must be a very great distance between the representatives and the people in general represented.

A small legislative body will fill with lawyers to the exclusion of farmers, and with so few representatives, only the views of "respectable characters" will be heard.

On the proposed plan, the state of Delaware, the city of Philadelphia, the state of Rhode Island, the province of Main, the county of Suffolk in Massachusetts will have one representative each; there can be but little personal knowledge, or but few communications, between him and the people at large of either of those districts. It has been observed, that mixing only with the respectable men, he will get the best information and ideas from them; he will also receive impressions favourable to their purposes particularly. Many plausible shifts have been made to divert the mind from dwelling on this defective representation, these I shall consider in another place. . . .

. . . We may amuse ourselves with names; but the fact is, men will be governed by the motives and temptations that surround their situation. Political evils to be guarded against are in the human character, and not in the name of patrician or plebian. Had the people of Italy, in the early period of the republic, selected yearly, or biennially, four or five hundred of their best informed men, emphatically from among themselves, these representatives would have formed an honest respectable assembly, capable of combining in them the views and exertions of the people, and their respectability would have procured them honest and able leaders, and we should have seen equal liberty established. True liberty stands in need of a fostering hand; from the days of Adam she has found but one temple to dwell in securely; she has laid the foundation of one, perhaps her last, in America; whether this is to be compleated and have duration, is yet a question. Equal liberty never yet found many advocates among the great: it is a disagreeable truth, that power perverts mens views in a greater degree, than public employments inform their understandings—they become hardened in certain maxims, and more lost to fellow feelings. Men may always be too cautious to commit alarming and glaring iniquities; but they, as well as systems, are liable to be corrupted by slow degrees. Junius well observes, we are, not only to guard against what men will do, but even against what they may do.[5] Men in high public offices are in stations where they gradually lose sight of the people, and do not often think of attending to them, except when necessary to answer private purposes.

> Public office invariably separates the officeholder from the constituent, and more is lost to corruption than is gained from experience.

The body of the people must have this true representative security placed some where in the nation; and in the United States, or in any extended empire, I am fully persuaded can be placed no where, but in the forms of a federal republic, where we can divide and place it in several state or district legislatures, giving the people in these the means of opposing heavy internal taxes and oppressive measures in the proper stages. A great empire contains the amities and animosities of a world within itself. We are not like the people of England, one people compactly settled on a small island, with a great city filled with frugal merchants, serving as a common centre of liberty and union: we are dispersed, and it is impracticable for any but the few to assemble

---

5. *The Letters of Junius*, I, letter 18.

in one place: the few must be watched, checked, and often resisted—tyranny has ever shewn a prediliction to be in close amity with them, or the one man. Drive it from kings and it flies to senators, to dicemvirs, to dictators, to tribunes, to popular leaders, to military chiefs, &c.

FROM *LETTER* 9

But "the people must elect good men:"—Examine the system, Is it practicable for them to elect fit and proper representatives where the number is so small? "But the people may chuse whom they please." This is an observation, I believe, made without due attention to facts and the state of the community. To explain my meaning, I will consider the descriptions of men commonly presented to the people as candidates for the offices of representatives—we may rank them in three classes: 1. The men who form the natural aristocracy, as before defined. 2. Popular demagogues: these men also are often politically elevated, so as to be seen by the people through the extent of large districts; they often have some abilities, without principle, and rise into notice by their noise and arts. 3. The substantial and respectable part of the democracy: they are a numerous and valuable set of men, who discern and judge well, but from being generally silent in public assemblies are often overlooked: they are the most substantial and best informed men in the several towns, who occasionally fill the middle grades of offices. &c. who hold not a splendid, but a respectable rank in private concerns: these men are extensively diffused through all the counties, towns, and small districts in the union; even they, and their immediate connections, are raised above the majority of the people, and as representatives are only brought to a level with a more numerous part of the community, the middle orders, and a degree nearer the mass of the people. Hence it is that the best practical representation, even in a small state, must be several degrees more aristocratical than the body of the people. A representation so formed as to admit but few or none of the third class, is, in my opinion, not deserving of the name—even in armies, courts-martial are so formed as to admit subaltern officers into them. The true idea is, so to open and enlarge the representation as to let in a due proportion of the third class with those of the first. Now, my opinion is, that the representation proposed is so small as that ordinarily very few

> Demagogues, generally elected in large voting districts, constitute a third class of representatives between natural aristocrats and natural democrats. (N.B.: Federalists suppose the opposite about district size.)

or none of them can be elected; and, therefore, after all the parade of words and forms the government must possess the soul of aristocracy, or something worse, the spirit of popular leaders.

I observed in a former letter, that the state of Delaware, of Rhode Island, the Province of Main, and each of the great counties in Massachusetts &c. would have one member, and rather more than one when the representatives shall be increased to one for each 30,000 inhabitants. In some districts the people are more dispersed and unequal than in others: In Delaware they are compact, in the Province of Main dispersed; how can the elections in either of those districts be regulated so as that a man of the third class can be elected? Exactly the same principles and motives, the same uncontroulable circumstances, must govern the elections as in the choice of the governors. Call upon the people of either of those districts to chuse a governor, and it will, probably, never happen that they will not bestow a major part, or the greatest number, of their votes on some very conspicuous or very popular character. A man that is known among a few thousands of people, may be quite unknown among thirty or forty thousand. On the whole, it appears to me to be almost a self-evident position, that when we call on thirty or forty thousand inhabitants to unite in giving their votes for one man, it will be uniformly impracticable for them to unite in any men, except those few who have become eminent for their civil or military rank, or their popular legal abilities: it will be found totally impracticable for men in the private walks of life, except in the profession of the law, to become conspicuous enough to attract the notice of so many electors and have their suffrages. . . .

We are not to expect even honest men rigidly to adhere to the line of strict impartiality, where the interest of themselves or friends is particularly concerned; if we do expect it, we shall deceive ourselves, and make a wrong estimate of human nature.

But it is asked how shall we remedy the evil, so as to complete and perpetuate the temple of equal laws and equal liberty? Perhaps we never can do it. Possibly we never may be able to do it in this immense country, under any one system of laws however modified; nevertheless, at present, I think the experiment worth a making. I feel an aversion to the disunion of the states, and to separate confederacies; the states have fought and bled in a common cause, and great dangers too may attend these confederacies. I think the system proposed capable of very considerable degrees of perfection, if we pursue first principles. . . . Our object is equal liberty, and equal laws diffusing their influence among all orders of men; to obtain this we must guard against the biass of interest and passions, against interested combinations, secret or open; we must aim at a balance of efforts and strength.

Clear it is, by increasing the representation we lessen the prospects of each member of congress being provided for in public offices; we proportionably lessen official influence and strengthen his prospects of becoming a private citizen, subject to the common burdens, without the compensation of the emoluments of office. By increasing the representation we make it more difficult to corrupt and influence the members; we diffuse them more extensively among the body of the people, perfect the balance, multiply information, strengthen the confidence of the people, and consequently support the laws on equal and free principles. . . .

BRUTUS

FROM *Essays*, 1787–88

The sixteen essays attributed to Brutus were published in The New-York Journal *between October 1787 and April 1788, largely coinciding with and responding to the* Federalist Papers. *Robert Yates was long thought to be Brutus, but a growing body of scholarship points to Melancton Smith or to someone associated with him. The selections from* Essays *1, 3, and 4 further explicate the Antifederalist view of representation.*

Source: Brutus, *Debate and Proceedings in the Convention of the Commonwealth of Massachusetts, Held in the Year 1788* (Boston: William White, Printer to the Commonwealth, 1856), pp. 374–76, 388–96 (with notes added and minor alterations made). (In 1856, the Massachusetts legislature ordered a new edition of the state's ratification debates; the edition was to include "a few of the more elaborate discussions in the public prints" [p. v]; the Brutus essays were among these "more elaborate discussions," placed in a chapter titled "Spirit of the Press.")

THOUGHT QUESTION: What are the advantages of having a large legislative body, especially a large lower chamber or House of Representatives?

FROM *ESSAY* 1

. . . In a free republic, although all laws are derived from the consent of the people, yet the people do not declare their consent by themselves in person, but by representatives, chosen by them, who are supposed to know the minds of their constituents, and to be possessed of integrity to declare this mind.

In every free government, the people must give their assent to the laws by which they are governed. This is the true criterion between a free government and an arbitrary one. The former are ruled by the will of the whole, expressed in any manner they may agree upon; the latter by the will of one, or a few. If the people are to give their assent to the laws, by persons chosen and appointed by them, the manner of the choice and ·the number chosen, must be such, as to possess, be disposed, and consequently qualified to declare the sentiments of the people; for if they do not know, or are not disposed to speak the sentiments of the people, the people do not govern, but the sovereignty is in a few. Now, in a large extended country, it is impossible to have a representation, possessing the sentiments, and of integrity, to declare the minds of the people, without having it so numerous and unwieldly, as to be subject in great measure to the inconveniency of a democratic government.

The territory of the United States is of vast extent; it now contains near three millions of souls, and is capable of containing much more than ten times that number. Is it practicable for a country, so large and so numerous as they will soon become, to elect a representation, that will speak their sentiments, without their becoming so numerous as to be incapable of transacting public business? It certainly is not.

In a republic, the manners, sentiments, and interests of the people should be similar. If this be not the case, there will be a constant clashing of opinions; and the representatives of one part will be continually striving against those of the other. This will retard the operations of government, and prevent such conclusions as will promote the public good. If we apply this remark to the condition of the United States, we shall be convinced that it forbids that we should be one government. The United States includes a variety of climates. The productions of the different parts of the union are very variant, and their interests, of consequence, diverse. Their manners and habits differ as much as their climates and productions; and their sentiments are by no means coincident. The laws and customs of the several states are, in many respects, very diverse, and in some opposite; each would be in favor of its own interests and customs, and, of consequence, a legislature, formed of representatives from the respective parts, would not only be too numerous

Representation applies to midsize republics only; for in small republics (city-states), the people govern directly, and in large republics (the United States consolidated into one great union), the dissimilarity of the parts precludes a common good. The implication is that the states, as midsize republics, must be the center of political life in America.

to act with any care or decision, but would be composed of such heterogenous and discordant principles, as would constantly be contending with each other.

The laws cannot be executed in a republic, of an extent equal to that of the United States, with promptitude.

The magistrates in every government must be supported in the execution of the laws, either by an armed force, maintained at the public expense for that purpose; or by the people turning out to aid the magistrate upon his command, in case of resistance.

In despotic governments, as well as in all the monarchies of Europe, standing armies are kept up to execute the commands of the prince or the magistrate, and are employed for this purpose when occasion requires: But they have always proved the destruction of liberty, and [are] abhorrent to the spirit of a free republic. In England, where they depend upon the parliament for their annual support, they have always been complained of as oppressive and unconstitutional, and are seldom employed in executing of the laws; never except on extraordinary occasions, and then under the direction of a civil magistrate.

People support laws passed by representatives resembling themselves; they resist laws passed by strangers purporting to be their "betters." A republic behaves like a despotism if law enforcement requires a standing army.

A free republic will never keep a standing army to execute its laws. It must depend upon the support of its citizens. But when a government is to receive its support from the aid of the citizens, it must be so constructed as to have the confidence, respect, and affection of the people. Men who, upon the call of the magistrate, offer themselves to execute the laws, are influenced to do it either by affection to the government, or from fear; where a standing army is at hand to punish offenders, every man is actuated by the latter principle, and therefore, when the magistrate calls, will obey: but, where this is not the case, the government must rest for its support upon the confidence and respect which the people have for their government and laws. The body of the people being attached, the government will always be sufficient to support and execute its laws, and to operate upon the fears of any faction which may be opposed to it, not only to prevent an opposition to the execution of the laws themselves, but also to compel the most of them to aid the magistrate; but the people will not be likely to have such confidence in their rulers, in a republic so extensive as the United States, as necessary for these purposes.

The confidence which the people have in their rulers, in a free republic, arises from their knowing them, from their being responsible to them for their conduct, and from the power they have of displacing them when they misbehave: but in a republic of the extent of this continent, the people in general would be acquainted with very few of their rulers: the people at large would know little of their proceedings, and it would be extremely difficult to change them. The people in Georgia and New Hampshire would not know one another's mind, and therefore could not act in concert to enable them to effect a general change of representatives. The different parts of so extensive a country could not possibly be made acquainted with the conduct of their representatives, nor be informed of the reasons upon which measures were founded. The consequence will be, they will have no confidence in their legislature, suspect them of ambitious views, be jealous of every measure they adopt, and will not support the laws they pass. Hence the government will be nerveless and inefficient, and no way will be left to render it otherwise, but by establishing an armed force to execute the laws at the point of the bayonet—a government of all others the most to be dreaded.

In a republic of such vast extent as the United-States, the legislature cannot attend to the various concerns and wants of its different parts. It cannot be sufficiently numerous to be acquainted with the local condition and wants of the different districts, and if it could, it is impossible it should have sufficient time to attend to and provide for all the variety of cases of this nature, that would be continually arising.

In so extensive a republic, the great officers of government would soon become above the control of the people, and abuse their power to the purpose of aggrandizing themselves, and oppressing them. The trust committed to the executive offices, in a country of the extent of the United States, must be various and of magnitude. The command of all the troops and navy of the republic, the appointment of officers, the power of pardoning offenses, the collecting of all the public revenues, and the power of expending them, with a number of other powers, must be lodged and exercised in every state, in the hands of a few. When these are attended with great honor and emolument, as they always will be in large states, so as greatly to interest men to pursue them, and to be proper objects for ambitious and designing men, such men will be ever restless in their pursuit after them. They will use the power, when they have acquired it, to the purposes of gratifying their own interest and ambition, and it is scarcely possible, in a very large republic, to call them to account for their misconduct, or to prevent their abuse of power. . . .

. . . It has been observed, that the happiness of society is the end of government—that every free government is founded in compact; and that, because it is impracticable for the whole community to assemble, or when assembled, to deliberate with wisdom, and decide with dispatch, the mode of legislating by representation was devised.

The very term, representative, implies, that the person or body chosen for this purpose, should resemble those who appoint them—representation of the people of America, if it be a true one, must be like the people. It ought to be so constituted, that a person, who is a stranger to the country, might be able to form a just idea of their character, by knowing that of their representatives. They are the sign—the people are the thing signified. It is absurd to speak of one thing being the representative of another, upon any other principle. The ground and reason of representation, in a free government, implies the same thing. Society instituted government to promote the happiness of the whole, and this is the great end always in view in the delegation of powers. It must then have been intended, that those who are placed instead of the people, should possess their sentiments and feelings, and be governed by their interests, or, in other words, should bear the strongest resemblance of those in whose room they are substituted.

It is obvious, that for an assembly to be a true likeness of the people of any country, they must be considerably numerous.—One man, or a few men, cannot possibly represent the feelings, opinions, and characters of a great multitude. In this respect, the new constitution is radically defective.—The house of assembly, which is intended as a representation of the people of America, will not, nor cannot, in the nature of things, be a proper one—sixty-five men[1] cannot be found in the United States, who hold the sentiments, possess the feelings, or are acquainted with the wants and interests of this vast country. This extensive continent is made up of a number of different classes of people; and to have a proper representation of them, each class

---

1. Article I, section 2, clause 3 of the Constitution reads: "The number of representatives shall not exceed one for every thirty thousand, but each State shall have at least one representative; and until such enumeration shall be made, the State of New Hampshire shall be entitled to choose three, Massachusetts eight, Rhode-Island and Providence Plantations one, Connecticut five, New-York six, New Jersey four, Pennsylvania eight, Delaware one, Maryland six, Virginia ten, North Carolina five, South Carolina five, and Georgia three." The sum is sixty-five, with six allotted to New York.

ought to have an opportunity of choosing their best informed men for the purpose; but this cannot possibly be the case in so small a number. The state of New York, on the present apportionment, will send six members to the assembly: I will venture to affirm, that number cannot be found in the state, who will bear a just resemblance to the several classes of people who compose it. In this assembly, the farmer, merchant, mechanic, and other various orders of people, ought to be represented according to their respective weight and numbers; and the representatives ought to be intimately acquainted with the wants, understand the interests of the several orders in the society, and feel a proper sense and becoming zeal to promote their prosperity. I cannot conceive that any six men in this state can be found properly qualified in these respects to discharge such important duties: but supposing it possible to find them, is there the least degree of probability that the choice of the people will fall upon such men?

According to the common course of human affairs, the natural aristocracy of the country will be elected. Wealth always creates influence, and this is generally much increased by large family connections: this class in society will forever have a great number of dependents; besides, they will always favor each other—it is their interest to combine—they will therefore constantly unite their efforts to procure men of their own rank to be elected—they will concenter all their force in every part of the state into one point, and by acting together, will most generally carry their election.

It is probable, that but few of the merchants, and those the most opulent and ambitious, will have a representation from their body—few of them are characters sufficiently conspicuous to attract the notice of the electors of the state in so limited a representation. The great body of the yeomen of the country cannot expect any of their order in this assembly—the station will be too elevated for them to aspire to—the distance between the people and their representatives, will be so very great, that there is no probability that a farmer, however respectable, will be chosen—the mechanics of every branch, must expect to be excluded from a seat in this Body.—It will and must be esteemed a station too high and exalted to be filled by any but the first men in the state, in point of fortune; so that in reality there will be no part of the people represented, but the rich, even in that branch of the legislature, which is called the democratic.—The well born, and highest orders in life, as they term themselves, will be ignorant of the sentiments of the middling class of citizens, strangers to their ability, wants, and difficulties, and void of sympathy, and fellow feeling.

This branch of the legislature will not only be an imperfect representation, but there will be no security in so small a body, against bribery, and corruption—It will consist at first, of sixty-five, and can never exceed one for every thirty thousand inhabitants; a majority of these, that is, thirty-three, are a quorum, and a majority of which, or seventeen, may pass any law—so that twenty-five men,[2] will have the power to give away all the property of the citizens of these states—what security therefore can there be for the people, where their liberties and property are at the disposal of so few men? It will literally be a government in the hands of the few to oppress and plunder the many.

> The lower house is too small (1) to give accurate represen-tation of the diverse interests of the popu-lation, (2) to prevent take over by the elite, (3) to guard against corruption within the body, and (4) to main-tain its independence from the executive.

You may conclude with a great degree of certainty, that it, like all others of a similar nature, will be managed by influence and corruption, and that the period is not far distant, when this will be the case, if it should be adopted; for even now there are some among us, whose characters stand high in the public estimation, and who have had a principal agency in framing this constitution, who do not scruple to say, that this is the only practicable mode of governing a people, who think with that degree of freedom which the Americans do—this government will have in their gift a vast number of offices of great honor and emolument. The members of the legislature are not excluded from appointments; and twenty-five of them, as the case may be, being secured, any measure may be carried.

The rulers of this country must be composed of very different materials from those of any other, of which history gives us any account, if the majority of the legislature are not, before many years, entirely at the devotion of the executive—and these states will soon be under the absolute domination of one, or a few, with the fallacious appearance of being governed by men of their own election.

The more I reflect on this subject, the more firmly am I persuaded, the representation is merely nominal—a mere burlesque; and that no security is

---

2. Who are these twenty-five? A Senate of twenty-six, with a quorum of fourteen, requires eight for a majority; these eight combine with seventeen representatives to pass a law. An extreme case is this to be sure, which in the event does not include the president.

provided against corruption and undue influence. No free people on earth, who have elected persons to legislate for them, ever reposed that confidence in so small a number. The British house of commons consists of five hundred and fifty-eight members; the number of inhabitants of Great-Britain, is computed at eight millions—this gives one member for a little more than fourteen thousand, which exceeds double the proportion this country can ever have [one per 30,000]; and yet we require a larger representation in proportion to our numbers, than Great-Britain, because this country is much more extensive, and differs more in its productions, interests, manners, and habits. The democratic branch of the legislatures of the several states in the union consists, I believe at present, of near two thousand; and this number was not thought too large for the security of liberty by the framers of our state constitutions: some of the states may have erred in this respect, but the difference between two thousand, and sixty-five, is so great, that it will bear no comparison. . . .

FROM *ESSAY* 4

There can be no free government where the people are not possessed of the power of making the laws by which they are governed, either in their own persons, or by others substituted in their stead.

Experience has taught mankind, that legislation by representatives is the most eligible, and the only practicable mode in which the people of any country can exercise this right, either prudently or beneficially. But then, it is a matter of the highest importance, in forming this representation, that it be so constituted as to be capable of understanding the true interests of the society for which it acts, and so disposed as to pursue the good and happiness of the people as its ultimate end. The object of every free government is the public good, and all lesser interests yield to it. That of every tyrannical government, is the happiness and aggrandizement of one, or a few, and to this the public felicity, and every other interest must submit.—The reason of this difference in these governments is obvious. The first is so constituted as to collect the views and wishes of the whole people in that of their rulers, while the latter is so framed as to separate the interests of the governors from that of the governed. The principle of self-love, therefore, that will influence the one to promote the good of the whole, will prompt the other to follow its own private advantage. The great art, therefore, in forming a good constitution, appears to be this, so to frame it, as that those to whom the power is committed shall be subject to the same feelings, and aim at the same objects as the people do, who transfer to them their authority. There is no possible way to effect this but by an equal, full and fair representation; this, therefore, is the great desideratum in politics. However fair an appearance any government may make, though it may possess a thousand plausible articles and be decorated with ever so many ornaments, yet if it is deficient in this essential principle of a full and just representation of the people, it will be only like a painted sepulcher.—For, without this it cannot be a free government; let the administration of it be good or ill, it still will be a government, not according to the will of the people, but according to the will of a few. . . .

The small number which is to compose this legislature, will not only expose it to the danger of that kind of corruption, and undue influence, which will arise from the gift of places of honor and emolument, or the more direct one of bribery, but it will also subject it to another kind of influence no less fatal to the liberties of the people, though it be not so flagrantly repugnant to the principles of rectitude. It is not to be expected that a legislature will be found in any country that will not have some of its members, who will pursue their private ends, and for which they will sacrifice the public good. Men of this character are, generally, artful and designing, and frequently possess brilliant talents and abilities: they commonly act in concert, and agree to share the spoils of their country among them; they will keep their object ever in view, and follow it with constancy. To effect their purpose, they will assume any shape and, Proteus like, mold themselves into any form—where they find members proof against direct bribery or gifts of offices, they will endeavor to mislead their minds by specious and false reasoning, to impose upon their unsuspecting honesty by an affectation of zeal for the public good; they will form juntos, and hold out-door meetings; they will operate upon the good nature of their opponents, by a thousand little attentions, and tease them into compliance by the earnestness of solicitation. Those who are acquainted with the manner of conducting business in public assemblies, know how prevalent art and address are in carrying a measure, even over men of the best intentions, and of good understanding.

The firmest security against this kind of improper and dangerous influence, as well as all other, is a strong and numerous representation: in such a house of assembly, so great a number must be gained over, before the private

> The principle of self-love refers here to the fact that human beings naturally seek their own good. To the degree that the people and their rulers are the same in opinions, passions, and interests, the good of the people, or the common good, is the good of the rulers, the two goods are sought as one, and the resulting government is just.

views of individuals could be gratified that there could be scarce a hope of success. But in the federal assembly [House of Representatives], seventeen men are all that is necessary to pass a law. It is probable, it will seldom happen that more than twenty-five will be requisite to form a majority, when it is considered what a number of places of honor and emolument will be in the gift of the executive, the powerful influence that great and designing men have over the honest and unsuspecting by their art and address, their soothing manners and civilities, and their cringing flattery, joined with their affected patriotism; when these different species of influence are combined, it is scarcely to be hoped that a legislature, composed of so small a number, as the one proposed by the new constitution, will long resist their force.

A farther objection against the feebleness of the representation is, that it will not possess the confidence of the people. The execution of the laws in a free government must rest on this confidence, and this must be founded on the good opinion they entertain of the framers of the laws. Every government must be supported, either by the people having such an attachment to it, as to be ready, when called upon, to support it, or by a force at the command of the government, to compel obedience. The latter mode destroys every idea of a free government; for the same force that may be employed to compel obedience to good laws, might, and probably would be used to wrest from the people their constitutional liberties. . . .

In order for the people safely to repose themselves on their rulers, they should not only be of their own choice. But it is requisite they should be acquainted with their abilities to manage the public concerns with wisdom. They should be satisfied that those who represent them are men of integrity, who will pursue the good of the community with fidelity; and will not be turned aside from their duty by private interest, or corrupted by undue influence; and that they will have such a zeal for the good of those whom they represent, as to excite them to be diligent in their service; but it is impossible the people of the United States should have sufficient knowledge of their representatives, when the numbers are so few, to acquire any rational satisfaction on either of these points. The people of this state will have very little acquaintance with those who may be chosen to represent them; a great part of them will, probably, not know the characters of their own members, much less that of a majority of those who will compose the federal assembly; they will consist of men, whose names they have never heard, and whose talents and regard for the public good, they are total strangers to; and they will have no persons so immediately of their choice so near them, of their neighbors and of their own rank in life, that they can feel themselves secure in trusting their interests in their hands.

The representatives of the people cannot, as they now do, after they have passed laws, mix with the people, and explain to them the motives which induced the adoption of any measure, point out its utility, and remove objections or silence unreasonable clamors against it.—The number will be so small that but a very few of the most sensible and respectable yeomanry of the country can ever have any knowledge of them: being so far removed from the people, their station will be elevated and important, and they will be considered as ambitious and designing. They will not be viewed by the people as part of themselves, but as a body distinct from them, and having separate interests to pursue; the consequence will be, that a perpetual jealousy will exist in the minds of the people against them; their conduct will be narrowly watched; their measures scrutinized; and their laws opposed, evaded, or reluctantly obeyed. This is natural, and exactly corresponds with the conduct of individuals towards those in whose hands they entrust important concerns. If the person confided in, be a neighbor with whom his employer is intimately acquainted, whose talents, he knows, are sufficient to manage the business with which he is charged, his honesty and fidelity unsuspected, and his friendship and zeal for the service of this principal unquestionable, he will commit his affairs into his hands with unreserved confidence, and feel himself secure; all the transactions of the agent will meet with the most favorable construction, and the measures he takes will give satisfaction. But, if the person employed be a stranger whom he has never seen, and whose character for ability or fidelity he cannot fully learn.—If he is constrained to choose him, because it was not in his power to procure one more agreeable to his wishes, he will trust him with caution, and be suspicious of all his conduct.

If then this government should not derive support from the good will of the people, it must be executed by force, or not executed at all; either case would lead to the total destruction of liberty.—The convention seemed aware of this, and have therefore provided for calling out the militia to execute the laws of the union [I.8.15]. If this system was so framed as to command that respect from the people, which every good free government will obtain, this provision was unnecessary—the people would support the civil magistrate. This power is a novel one, in free governments—these have depended for the execution of the laws on the Posse

Comitatus,[3] and never raised an idea, that the people would refuse to aid the civil magistrate in executing those laws they themselves had made. . . .

3. *Posse Comitatus* (Latin for "force of the county") is an irregular party of citizens organized by local authorities to pursue a felon or put down a riot.

FROM Debates of the New York State Ratifying Convention, 1788

The convention sat from June 17 to July 26, 1788. After first hearing from Chancellor Robert Livingston and John Lansing, each offering expansive opening statements, the convention agreed to a provision-by-provision review of the Constitution and quickly settled in on Article I, section 2, clauses 1 and 3: the term of office and apportionment of representatives and the size of the lower house. The first selection reprinted here is taken from a June 21 exchange between Melancton Smith, speaking for the Antifederalists, and Alexander Hamilton, speaking for the Federalists. The second selection is taken from the June 24–25 debates on Article I, section 3, clauses 1 and 2: the organization of the upper house. The focus here is on a proposed amendment by Gilbert Livingston to add rotation and recall of senators to the Constitution. Speaking in response are Robert Livingston, Smith, and Hamilton.

Source: Jonathan Elliot, ed., *The Debates in the Several State Conventions on the Adoption of the Federal Constitution as Recommended by the General Convention at Philadelphia, in 1787*, vol. 2 (New York: Burt Franklin, 1888), pp. 243–59, 286–89, 291–93, 309–21 (with notes added and minor alterations made).

THOUGHT QUESTION: Who make the best republican citizens, natural aristocrats or yeoman farmers, and are they best because of their virtues or their vices?

JUNE 21

Mr. M. SMITH. I had the honor, yesterday, of submitting an amendment to the clause under consideration, with some observations in support of it.[1] I hope

1. On June 20 Smith proposed an amendment to I.2.3 and its cap of one representative per 30,000 inhabitants. The amendment read: "*Resolved*, That it is proper that the number of representatives be fixed at the rate of one for every twenty thousand inhabitants, to be ascertained on the principles mentioned in the 2nd section of the 1st article of the Constitution, until they amount to three hundred; after which they shall be apportioned among the states, in proportion to the number of inhabitants of the states respectively; and that, before the first enumeration shall be made [census taken], the several states shall be entitled to choose double the number of representatives [130 instead of 65], for that purpose mentioned in the Constitution."

I shall be indulged in making some additional remarks in reply to what has been offered by the honorable gentleman [Alexander Hamilton] from New York. . . .

The honorable gentleman says, that the clause, by obvious construction, fixes the representation. I wish not to torture words or sentences. I perceive no such obvious construction.

I see clearly that, on one hand, the representatives cannot exceed one for thirty thousand inhabitants; and, on the other, that whatever larger number of inhabitants may be taken for the rule of apportionment, each state shall be entitled to send one representative. Everything else appears to me in the discretion of the legislature. If there be any other limitation, it is certainly implied. Matters of moment should not be left to doubtful construction. It is urged that the number of representatives will be fixed at one for thirty thousand, because it will be the interest of the larger states to do it. I cannot discern the force of this argument. To me it appears clear, that the relative weight of influence of the different states will be the same, with the number of representatives at sixty-five as at six hundred, and that of the individual members greater; for each member's share of power will decrease as the number of the House of Representatives increases. If, therefore, this maxim be true, that men are unwilling to relinquish powers which they once possess, we are not to expect the House of Representatives will be inclined to enlarge the numbers. The same motive will operate to influence the President and Senate to oppose the increase of the number of representatives; for, in proportion as the House of Representatives is augmented, they will feel their own power diminished. It is, therefore, of the highest importance that a suitable number of representatives should be established by the Constitution. . . .

> The Constitution should mandate increases in the size of the House of Representatives; for neither large states nor incumbent congressmen will have an interest in maintaining the one per 30,000 ratio.

But an honorable gentleman has observed, that it is a problem that cannot be solved, what the proper number is which ought to compose the House of Representatives, and calls upon me to fix the number. I admit that this is a question that will not admit of a solution with mathematical certainty; few political questions will; yet we may determine with certainty that certain numbers are too small or too large. We may be sure that ten is too small, and a thousand too large a number. Everyone will allow that the first number is too small to possess the sentiments, be influenced by the interests of the people, or secure against corruption; a thousand would be too numerous to be capable of deliberating.

FROM Debates of the New York State Ratifying Convention, 1788

To determine whether the number of representatives proposed by this Constitution is sufficient, it is proper to examine the qualifications which this house ought to possess, in order to exercise their power discreetly for the happiness of the people. The idea that naturally suggests itself to our minds, when we speak of representatives, is, that they resemble those they represent. They should be a true picture of the people, possess a knowledge of their circumstances and their wants, sympathize in all their distresses, and be disposed to seek their true interests. The knowledge necessary for the representative of a free people not only comprehends extensive political and commercial information, such as is acquired by men of refined education, who have leisure to attain to high degrees of improvement, but it should also comprehend that kind of acquaintance with the common concerns and occupations of the people, which men of the middling class of life are, in general, more competent to than those of a superior class. To understand the true commercial interests of a country, not only requires just ideas of the general commerce of the world, but also, and principally, a knowledge of the productions of your own country, and their value, what your soil is capable of producing, the nature of your manufactures, and the capacity of the country to increase both. To exercise the power of laying taxes, duties, and excises, with discretion, requires something more than an acquaintance with the abstruse parts of the system of finance. It calls for a knowledge of the circumstances and ability of the people in general—a discernment how the burdens imposed will bear upon the different classes.

From these observations results this conclusion—that the number of representatives should be so large, as that, while it embraces the men of the first class, it should admit those of the middling class of life. I am convinced that this government is so constituted that the representatives will generally be composed of the first class in the community, which I shall distinguish by the name of the *natural aristocracy* of the country. I do not mean to give offence by using this term. I am sensible this idea is treated by many gentlemen as chimerical. I shall be asked what is meant by the *natural aristocracy*, and told that no such distinction of classes of men exists among us. It is true, it is our singular felicity that we have no legal or hereditary distinctions of this kind; but still there are real differences. Every society naturally divides itself into classes. The Author of nature has bestowed on some greater capacities than others; birth, education, talents, and wealth, create distinctions among men as visible, and of as much influence, as titles, stars, and garters. In every society, men of this class will command a superior degree of respect; and if the government is so constituted as to admit but few to exercise the powers of it, it will, according to the natural course of things, be in their hands. Men in the middling class, who are qualified as representatives, will not be so anxious to be chosen as those of the first. When the number is so small, the office will be highly elevated and distinguished; the style in which the members live will probably be high; circumstances of this kind will render the place of a representative not a desirable one to sensible, substantial men, who have been used to walk in the plain and frugal paths of life.

Besides, the influence of the great will generally enable them to succeed in elections. It will be difficult to combine a district of country containing thirty or forty thousand inhabitants—frame your election laws as you please—in any other character, unless it be in one of conspicuous military, popular, civil, or legal talents. The great easily form associations; the poor and middling class form them with difficulty. If the elections be by plurality[2]—as probably will be the case in this state—it is almost certain none but the great will be chosen, for they easily unite their interests: the common people will divide, and their divisions will be promoted by the others. There will be scarcely a chance of their uniting in any other but some great man, unless in some popular demagogue, who will probably be destitute of principle. A substantial yeoman, of sense and discernment, will hardly ever be chosen.

From these remarks, it appears that the government will fall into the hands of the few and the great. This will be a government of oppression. I do not mean to declaim against the great and charge them indiscriminately with want of principle and honesty. The same passions and prejudices govern

All societies divide between the great, called the "natural aristocracy," and the middling class. The former enjoy electoral advantages but are ill-equipped, or are unwilling, to represent the latter, whose life circumstances and modest ambitions actually make them better citizens. Election of the middling sort is, therefore, a democratic imperative, and a large lower house is the means by which that goal is accomplished.

---

2. *Plurality* here means statewide, at-large elections where the top six vote getters are elected (the Constitution allots an initial six representatives to New York). District voting is the alternative (i.e., the state divided into six districts, each with its own representative). Under the Constitution, state legislatures make these determinations (I.4.1). (See p. 33, n. 5, in this game book.)

all men. The circumstances in which men are placed in a great measure give a cast to the human character. Those in middling circumstances have less temptation; they are inclined by habit, and the company with whom they associate, to set bounds to their passions and appetites. If this is not sufficient, the want of means to gratify them will be a restraint: they are obliged to employ their time in their respective callings; hence the substantial yeomanry of the country are more temperate, of better morals, and less ambition, than the great. The latter do not feel for the poor and middling class; the reasons are obvious—they are not obliged to use the same pains and labor to procure property as the other. They feel not the inconveniences arising from the payment of small sums. The great consider themselves above the common people, entitled to more respect, do not associate with them; they fancy themselves to have a right of preeminence in everything. In short, they possess the same feelings, and are under the influence of the same motives, as an hereditary nobility.

I know the idea that such a distinction exists in this country is ridiculed by some; but I am not the less apprehensive of danger from their influence on this account. Such distinctions exist all the world over, have been taken notice of by all writers on free government, and are founded in the nature of things. It has been the principal care of free governments to guard against the encroachments of the great. Common observation and experience prove the existence of such distinctions. Will anyone say that there does not exist in this country the pride of family, of wealth, of talents, and that they do not command influence and respect among the common people? [. . .] We ought to guard against the government being placed in the hands of this class. They cannot have that sympathy with their constituents which is necessary to connect them closely to their interests. Being in the habit of profuse living, they will be profuse in the public expenses. They find no difficulty in paying their taxes, and therefore do not feel public burdens. Besides, if they govern, they will enjoy the emoluments of the government. The middling class, from their frugal habits, and feeling themselves the public burdens, will be careful how they increase them.

But I may be asked, Would you exclude the first class in the community from any share in legislation? I answer, By no means. They would be factious, discontented, and constantly disturbing the government. It would also be unjust. They have their liberties to protect, as well as others, and the largest share of property. But my idea is, that the Constitution should be so framed as to admit this class, together with a sufficient number of the middling class to control them. You will then combine the abilities and honesty of the community, a proper degree of information, and a disposition to pursue the public good. A representative body, composed principally of respectable yeomanry, is the best possible security to liberty. When the interest of this part of the community is pursued, the public good is pursued, because the body of every nation consists of this class, and because the interest of both the rich and the poor are involved in that of the middling class. No burden can be laid on the poor but what will sensibly affect the middling class. Any law rendering property insecure would be injurious to them. When, therefore, this class in society pursue their own interest, they promote that of the public, for it is involved in it.

> The poor constitute a third class, and it is a further recommendation of the middling class that they mediate between the rich and the poor.

In so small a number of representatives, there is great danger from corruption and combination. A great politician has said that every man has his price. I hope this is not true in all its extent; but I ask the gentleman to inform me what government there is in which it has not been practiced. Notwithstanding all that has been said of the defects in the constitution of the ancient confederacies in the Grecian republics, their destruction is to be imputed more to this cause than to any imperfection in their forms of government. This was the deadly poison that effected their dissolution. This is an extensive country, increasing in population and growing in consequence. Very many lucrative offices will be in the grant of the government, which will be objects of avarice and ambition. How easy will it be to gain over a sufficient number, in the bestowment of offices, to promote the views and the purposes of those who grant them!

Foreign corruption is also to be guarded against. A system of corruption is known to be the system of government in Europe. It is practiced without blushing; and we may lay it to our account, it will be attempted amongst us. The most effectual as well as natural security against this is a strong democratic branch in the legislature, frequently chosen, including in it a number of the substantial, sensible yeomanry of the country. Does the House of Representatives answer this description? I confess, to me they hardly wear the complexion of a democratic branch; they appear the mere shadow of representation. The whole number, in both houses, amounts to ninety-one; of these forty-six make a quorum; and twenty-four of those, being secured, may carry any point.[3] Can the liberties of three millions of people be securely trusted in the hands of twenty-four men? Is it prudent to commit to so small a number the decision of the great questions which will come before them? Reason revolts at the idea.

The honorable gentleman from New York has said, that sixty-five members in the House of Representatives are sufficient for the present situation of the country; and, taking it for granted that they will increase as one for thirty thousand, in twenty-five years they will amount to two hundred. It is admitted, by this observation, that the number fixed in the Constitution is not sufficient without it is augmented. It is not declared that an increase shall be made, but is left at the discretion of the legislature, by the gentleman's own concession; therefore the Constitution is imperfect.

Depending on the virtue of the people to guard the Constitution is tantamount to having no Constitution at all.

We certainly ought to fix, in the Constitution, those things which are essential to liberty. If anything falls under this description, it is the number of the legislature. To say, as this gentleman does, that our security is to depend upon the spirit of the people, who will be watchful of their liberties, and not suffer them to be infringed, is absurd. It would equally prove that we might adopt any form of government. I believe, were we to create a despot; he would not immediately dare to act the tyrant; but it would not be long before he would destroy the spirit of the people, or the people would destroy him. If our people have a high sense of liberty, the government should be congenial to this spirit, calculated to cherish the love of liberty, while yet it had sufficient force to restrain licentiousness. Government operates upon the spirit of the people, as well as the spirit of the people operates upon it; and if they are not conformable to each other, the one or the other will prevail.

In a less time than twenty-five years, the government will receive its tone. What the spirit of the country may be at the end of that period, it is impossible to foretell. Our duty is to frame a government friendly to liberty

---

3. Smith says that twenty-four makes a quorum, whereas Brutus says twenty-five (*Essay* 3). Brutus is correct, because quorums are made separately, not in combination (I.5.1): a majority of sixty-five (House) is thirty-three, and a majority of thirty-three is seventeen; while a majority of twenty-six (Senate) is fourteen, and a majority of fourteen is eight; $17 + 8 = 25$. Smith takes a majority of ninety-one (House and Senate combined) to get forty-six, and a majority of forty-six to get twenty-four.

and the rights of mankind, which will tend to cherish and cultivate a love of liberty among our citizens. If this government becomes oppressive, it will be by degrees: it will aim at its end by disseminating sentiments of government opposite to republicanism and proceed from step to step in depriving the people of a share in the government. A recollection of the change that has taken place in the minds of many in this country in the course of a few years, ought to put us on our guard.

Many, who are ardent advocates for the new system, reprobate republican principles as chimerical, and such as ought to be expelled from society. Who would have thought, ten years ago, that the very men, who risked their lives and fortunes in support of republican principles, would now treat them as the fictions of fancy? A few years ago, we fought for liberty; we framed a general government on free principles; we placed the state legislatures, in whom the people have a full and a fair representation, between Congress and the people. We were then, it is true, too cautious, and too much restricted the powers of the general government. But now it is proposed to go into the contrary, and a more dangerous extreme—to remove all barriers, to give the new government free access to our pockets, and ample command of our persons, and that without providing for a genuine and fair representation of the people.

No one can say what the progress of the change of sentiment may be in twenty-five years. The same men who now cry up the necessity of an energetic government, to induce a compliance with this system, may, in much less time, reprobate this in as severe terms as they now do the Confederation, and may as strongly urge the necessity of going as far beyond this as this is beyond the Confederation. Men of this class are increasing: they have influence, talents, and industry. It is time to form a barrier against them. And while we are willing to establish a government adequate to the purposes of the Union, let us be careful to establish it on the broad basis of equal liberty.

Mr. HAMILTON then resumed his argument. When, said he, I had the honor to address the committee yesterday, I gave a history of the circumstances which attended the Convention, when forming the plan before you. I endeavored to point out to you the principles of accommodation on which this arrangement was made, and to show that the contending interests of the states led them to establish the representation as it now stands.[4] In the second place, I attempted to prove that, in point of number, the representation would be perfectly secure.

Sir, no man agrees more perfectly than myself to the main principle for which the gentlemen contend. I agree that there should be a broad democratic branch in the national legislature. But this matter, sir, depends on circumstances. It is impossible, in the first instance, to be precise and exact with regard to the number; and it is equally impossible to determine to what point it may be proper in future to increase it. On this ground I am disposed to acquiesce. In my reasonings on this subject of government, I rely more on the interests and opinions of men, than on any speculative parchment provisions whatever. I have found that constitutions are more or less excellent as they are more or less agreeable to the natural operation of things. I am, therefore, disposed not to dwell long on curious speculations, or pay much attention to modes and forms; but to adopt a system whose principles have been sanctioned by experience, adapt it to the real state of our country, and depend on probable reasonings for its operation and result.

I contend that sixty-five and twenty-six, in two bodies, afford perfect security, in the present state of things; and that the regular progressive enlargement, which was in the contemplation of the general Convention, will leave not an apprehension of danger in the most timid and suspicious mind. It will be the interest of the large states to increase the representation. This will be the standing instruction to their delegates. But, say the gentlemen, the members of Congress will be interested not to increase the number, as it will diminish their relative influence. In all their reasoning upon this subject, there seems to be this fallacy: They suppose that the representative will have no motive of action, on the one side, but a sense of duty; or on the other, but corruption. They do not reflect that he is to return to the community; that he is dependent on the will of the people, and that it cannot be his interest to oppose their wishes. Sir, the general sense of the people will regulate the conduct of their representatives. I admit that there are exceptions to this rule: there are certain conjunctures, when it may be necessary and proper to disregard the opinions which the majority of the people have formed. But,

---

4. Hamilton is referring to the compromises worked out between navigating and non-navigating states, between large and small states, and between free and slave states.

in the general course of things, the popular views, and even prejudices, will direct the actions of the rulers. . . .

. . . Sir, if I believed that the number would remain at sixty-five, I confess I should give my vote for an amendment, though in a different form from the one proposed.[5]

The amendment proposes a ratio of one for twenty thousand. I would ask by what rule or reasoning it is determined that one man is a better representative for twenty than thirty thousand. At present we have three millions of people; in twenty-five years, we shall have six millions; and in forty years, nine millions. And this is a short period, as it relates to the existence of states. Here, then, according to the ratio of one for thirty thousand, we shall have, in forty years, three hundred representatives. If this be true, and if this be a safe representation, why be dissatisfied? Why embarrass the Constitution with amendments that are merely speculative and useless?

I agree with the gentleman, that a very small number might give some color for suspicion. I acknowledge that ten would be unsafe; on the other hand, a thousand would be too numerous. But I ask him, Why will not ninety-one be an adequate and safe representation? This, at present, appears to be the proper medium. Besides, the President of the United States will be himself the representative of the people. From the competition that ever subsists between the branches of government, the President will be induced to protect their rights, whenever they are invaded by either branch. On whatever side we view this subject, we discover various and powerful checks to the encroachments of Congress. The true and permanent interests of the members are opposed to corruption. Their number is vastly too large for easy combination. The rivalship between the houses will forever prove an insuperable obstacle. The people have an obvious and powerful protection in their state governments. Should anything dangerous be attempted, these bodies of perpetual observation will be capable of forming and conducting plans of regular opposition. Can we suppose the people's love of liberty will not, under the incitement of their legislative leaders, be roused into resistance, and the madness of tyranny be extinguished at a blow? Sir, the danger is too distant; it is beyond all rational calculations.

> The Constitution contains such institutional safeguards as an independent executive branch, a bicameral legislative branch, and state governments. Safety does not depend solely on the virtue and vigilance of the people.

---

5. The proposed amendment is Smith's quoted earlier.

It has been observed, by an honorable gentleman, that a pure democracy, if it were practicable, would be the most perfect government. Experience has proved that no position in politics is more false than this. The ancient democracies, in which the people themselves deliberated, never possessed one feature of good government. Their very character was tyranny; their figure, deformity. When they assembled, the field of debate presented an ungovernable mob, not only incapable of deliberation, but prepared for every enormity. In these assemblies, the enemies of the people brought forward their plans of ambition systematically. They were opposed by their enemies of another party; and it became a matter of contingency, whether the people subjected themselves to be led blindly by one tyrant or by another.

It was remarked yesterday, that a numerous representation was necessary to obtain the confidence of the people. This is not generally true. The confidence of the people will easily be gained by a good administration. This is the true touchstone. . . . Massachusetts has three hundred representatives; New York has sixty-five. Have the people in this state less confidence in their representation than the people of that? Delaware has twenty-one. Do the inhabitants of New York feel a higher confidence than those of Delaware? I have stated these examples to prove that the gentleman's principle is not just. The popular confidence depends on circumstances very distinct from considerations of number. Probably the public attachment is more strongly secured by a train of prosperous events, which are the result of wise deliberation and vigorous execution, and to which large bodies are much less competent than small ones. If the representative conducts with propriety, he will necessarily enjoy the good-will of the constituent. It appears, then, if my reasoning be just, that the clause is perfectly proper, upon the principles of the gentleman who contends for the amendment; as there is in it the greatest degree of present security, and a moral certainty of an increase equal to our utmost wishes.

It has been further, by the gentlemen in the opposition, observed, that a large representation is necessary to understand the interests of the people. This principle is by no means true in the extent to which the gentlemen seem to carry it. I would ask, Why may not a man understand the interests of thirty as well as of twenty? The position appears to be made upon the unfounded presumption that all the interests of all parts of the community must be represented. No idea is more erroneous than this. Only such interests are proper to be represented as are involved in the powers of the general government.

These interests come completely under the observation of one or a few men; and the requisite information is by no means augmented in proportion to the increase of number.

What are the objects of the government? Commerce, taxation, &c. In order to comprehend the interests of commerce, is it necessary to know how wheat is raised, and in what proportion it is produced in one district and in another? By no means. Neither is this species of knowledge necessary in general calculations upon the subject of taxation. The information necessary for these purposes is that which is open to every intelligent inquirer, and of which five men may be as perfectly possessed as fifty. In royal governments, there are usually particular men to whom the business of taxation is committed. These men have the forming of systems of finance and the regulation of the revenue. I do not mean to commend this practice. It proves, however, this point—that a few individuals may be competent to these objects, and that large numbers are not necessary to perfection in the science of taxation.

But grant, for a moment, that this minute and local knowledge the gentlemen contend for is necessary; let us see if, under the new Constitution, it will not probably be found in the representation. The natural and proper mode of holding elections will be, to divide the state into districts, in proportion to the number to be elected.[6] This state will consequently be divided, at first, into six. One man from each district will probably possess all the knowledge gentlemen can desire.

Are the senators of this state more ignorant of the interests of the people than the Assembly? Have they not ever enjoyed their confidence as much? Yet, instead of six districts, they are elected in four; and the chance of their being collected from the smaller divisions of the state consequently diminishes. Their number is but twenty-four;[7] and their powers are coextensive with those of the Assembly and reach objects which are most dear to the people—life, liberty, and property.

Sir, we hear constantly a great deal which is rather calculated to awake our passions, and create prejudices, than to conduct us to the truth, and teach us our real interests. I do not suppose this to be the design of the gentlemen.

6. Hamilton disputes Smith's supposition that House elections will be at-large.
7. New York has twenty-four senators elected from four districts, thus six senators from each (where the election is by plurality vote).

Why, then, are we told so often of an aristocracy? For my part, I hardly know the meaning of this word, as it is applied. If all we hear be true, this government is really a very bad one. But who are the aristocracy among us? Where do we find men elevated to a perpetual rank above their fellow-citizens, and possessing powers entirely independent of them? The arguments of the gentlemen only go to prove that there are men who are rich, men who are poor, some who are wise, and others who are not; that, indeed, every distinguished man is an aristocrat. This reminds me of a description of the aristocrats I have seen in a late publication styled the Federal Farmer. The author reckons in the aristocracy all governors of states, members of Congress, chief magistrates, and all officers of the militia [*Letter* 7 on p. 58]. This description, I presume to say, is ridiculous. The image is a phantom. Does the new government render a rich man more eligible than a poor one? No. It requires no such qualification. It is bottomed on the broad and equal principle of your state constitution.

Sir, if the people have it in their option to elect their most meritorious men, is this to be considered as an objection? Shall the Constitution oppose their wishes, and abridge their most invaluable privilege? While property continues to be pretty equally divided, and a considerable share of information pervades the community, the tendency of the people's suffrages will be to elevate merit even from obscurity. As riches increase and accumulate in few hands, as luxury prevails in society, virtue will be in a greater degree considered as only a graceful appendage of wealth, and the tendency of things will be to depart from the republican standard. This is the real disposition of human nature: it is what neither the honorable member nor myself can correct; it is a common misfortune, that awaits our state constitution as well as all others.

Material progress brings moral decline, corroding the springs of republican government.

There is an advantage incident to large districts of election, which perhaps the gentlemen, amidst all their apprehensions of influence and bribery, have not adverted to. In large districts, the corruption of the electors is much more difficult; combinations for the purposes of intrigue are less easily formed; factions and cabals are little known. In a small district, wealth will have a more complete influence, because the people in the vicinity of a great man are more immediately his dependents, and because this influence has fewer objects to act upon. . . .

Large electoral districts provide an additional check on powerful individuals attempting to bribe and corrupt the electorate.

It is a harsh doctrine that men grow wicked in proportion as they improve and enlighten their minds. Experience has by no means justified us in the supposition that there is more virtue in one class of men than in another. Look through the rich and the poor of the community, the learned and the ignorant. Where does virtue predominate? The difference indeed consists, not in the quantity, but kind, of vices which are incident to various classes; and here the advantage of character belongs to the wealthy. Their vices are probably more favorable to the prosperity of the state than those of the indigent, and partake less of moral depravity.

> The ambition of the few is more socially advantageous than the envy of the many.

After all, sir, we must submit to this idea, that the true principle of a republic is, that the people should choose whom they please to govern them. Representation is imperfect in proportion as the current of popular favor is checked. This great source of free government, popular election, should be perfectly pure, and the most unbounded liberty allowed. Where this principle is adhered to; where, in the organization of the government, the legislative, executive, and judicial branches are rendered distinct; where, again, the legislature is divided into separate houses, and the operations of each are controlled by various checks and balances, and, above all, by the vigilance and weight of the stale governments—to talk of tyranny, and the subversion of our liberties, is to speak the language of enthusiasm.

This balance between the national and state governments ought to be dwelt on with peculiar attention, as it is of the utmost importance. It forms a double security to the people. If one encroaches on their rights, they will find a powerful protection in the other. Indeed, they will both be prevented from overpassing their constitutional limits, by a certain rivalship, which will ever subsist between them. I am persuaded that a firm union is as necessary to perpetuate our liberties as it is to make us respectable; and experience will probably prove that the national government will be as natural a guardian of our freedom as the state legislature themselves. . . .

We have been told that the spirit of patriotism and love of liberty are almost extinguished among the people, and that it has become a prevailing doctrine that republican principles ought to be hooted out of the world. Sir, I am confident that such remarks as these are rather occasioned by the heat of argument than by a cool conviction of their truth and justice. As far as my experience has extended, I have heard no such doctrine; nor have I discovered any diminution of regard for those rights and liberties, in defense of which the people have fought and suffered. There have been, undoubtedly, some men who have had speculative doubts on the subject of government; but the principles of republicanism are founded on too firm a basis to be shaken by a few speculative and skeptical reasoners. Our error has been of a very different kind. We have erred through excess of caution, and a zeal false and impracticable. Our counsels have been destitute of consistency and stability. I am flattered with the hope, sir, that we have now found a cure for the evils under which we have so long labored. I trust that the proposed Constitution affords a genuine specimen of representative and republican government, and that it will answer, in an eminent degree, all the beneficial purposes of society.

JUNE 24

MR. G. LIVINGSTON. He, in the first place, considered the importance of the *Senate* as a branch of the legislature, in three points of view: —

First, they would possess legislative powers coextensive with those of the House of Representatives except with respect to originating revenue laws; which, however, they would have power to reject or amend, as in the case of other bills. Secondly, they would have an importance, even exceeding that of the representative house, as they would be composed of a smaller number, and possess more firmness and system. Thirdly, their consequence and dignity would still further transcend those of the other branch, from their longer continuance in office. These powers, Mr. Livingston contended, rendered the Senate a dangerous body.

He went on, in the second place, to enumerate and animadvert on [criticize] the powers with which they were clothed in their judicial capacity, and in their capacity of council to the President, and in the forming of treaties. In the last place, as if too much power could not be given to this body, they were made, he said, a council of appointment, by whom ambassadors and other officers of state were to be appointed. These are the powers, continued he, which are vested in this small body of twenty-six men; in some cases, to be exercised by a bare quorum, which is fourteen; a majority of which number, again, is eight. What are the checks provided to balance this great mass of power? Our present Congress cannot serve longer than three years in six: they are at any time subject to recall. These and other checks were considered as necessary at a period which I choose to honor with the name of *virtuous*. Sir,

I venerate the spirit with which every thing was done at the trying time in which the Confederation was formed. America had then a sufficiency of this virtue to resolve to resist perhaps the first nation in the universe, even unto bloodshed. What was her aim? Equal liberty and safety. What ideas had she of this equal liberty? Read them in her Articles of Confederation. True it is, sir, there are some powers wanted to make this glorious compact complete. But, sir, let us be cautious that we do not err more on the other hand, by giving power too profusely, when, perhaps, it will be too late to recall it.

Consider, sir, the great influence which this body, armed at all points, will have. What will be the effect of this? Probably a security of their re-election, as long as they please. Indeed, in my view, it will amount nearly to an appointment for life. What will be their situation in a federal town? Hallowed ground! Nothing so unclean as state laws to enter there, surrounded, as they will be, by an impenetrable wall of adamant and gold, the wealth of the whole country flowing into it. [Here a member, who did not fully understand, called out to know what WALL the gentleman meant; on which he turned, and replied, "A wall of gold—of adamant, which will flow in from all parts of the continent." At which flowing metaphor, a great laugh in the house.] The gentleman continued: Their attention to their various business will probably require their constant attendance. In this Eden will they reside with their families, distant from the observation of the people. In such a situation, men are apt to forget their dependence, lose their sympathy, and contract selfish habits. Factions are apt to be formed, if the body becomes permanent. The senators will associate only with men of their own class, and thus become strangers to the condition of the common people. They should not only return, and be obliged to live with the people, but return to their former rank of citizenship, both to revive their sense of dependence, and to gain a knowledge of the country. This will afford opportunity to bring forward the genius and information of the states, and will be a stimulus to acquire political abilities. It will be the means of diffusing a more general knowledge of the measures and spirit of the administration. These things will confirm the people's confidence in government. When they see those who have been high in office residing among them as private citizens, they will feel more forcibly that the government is of their own choice. The members of this branch having the idea impressed on their minds, that they are soon to return to the level whence the suffrages of the people raised them,—this good effect will follow: they will consider their interests as the same with those of their constituents, and that they legislate for themselves as well as others. They will not conceive themselves made to receive, enjoy, and rule, nor the people solely to earn, pay, and submit.

Mr. Chairman, I have endeavored, with as much perspicuity and candor as I am master of, shortly to state my objections to this clause. I would wish the committee to believe that they are not raised for the sake of opposition, but that I am very sincere in my sentiments in this important investigation. The Senate, as they are now constituted, have little or no check on them. Indeed, sir, too much is put into their hands. When we come to that part of the system which points out their powers, it will be the proper time to consider this subject more particularly.

I think, sir, we must relinquish the idea of safety under this government, if the time for services is not further limited, and the power of recall given to the state legislatures. I am strengthened in my opinion by an observation made yesterday, by an honorable member from New York, to this effect—"that there should be no fear of corruption of the members in the House of Representatives; especially as they are, in two years, to return to the body of the people." I therefore move that the committee adopt the following resolution, as an amendment to this clause: —

"**Resolved**, That no person shall be eligible as a senator for more than six years in any term of twelve years, and that it shall be in the power of the legislatures of the several states to recall their senators, or either of them, and to elect others in their stead, to serve for the remainder of the time for which such senator or senators, so recalled, were appointed."

Mr. R. R. LIVINGSTON. The amendment appears to have in view two objects—that a rotation shall be established in the Senate, and that its members shall be subject to recall by the state legislatures. It is not contended that six years are too long a time for the senators to remain in office. Indeed, this cannot be objected to, when the purposes for which this body is instituted are considered. They are to form treaties with foreign nations. This requires a comprehensive knowledge of foreign politics, and an extensive acquaintance with characters, whom, in this capacity, they have to negotiate with, together with such an intimate conception of our best interests, relative to foreign powers, as can only be derived from much experience in this business. What singular policy, to cut off the hand which has just qualified itself for action! But, says the gentleman, as they are the representatives of the states, those states have a control. Will this principle hold good? The members of the lower house are the representatives of the people. Have the people any power to recall them? What would be the tendency of the power contended for? Clearly this: The state legislatures, being frequently subject to factious and irregular passions, may be unjustly disaffected and discontented with their delegates; and a senator may be appointed one day and recalled the next. This would be a source of endless confusion. The Senate are indeed designed to represent the state governments; but they are also the representatives of the United States, and are not to consult the interest of any one state alone, but that of the Union. This could never be done, if there was a power of recall; for sometimes it happens that small sacrifices are absolutely indispensable for the good and safety of the confederacy; but, if a senator should presume to consent to these sacrifices, he would be immediately recalled. This reasoning turns on the idea that a state, not being able to comprehend the interest of the whole, would, in all instances, adhere to her own, even to the hazard of the Union.

I should disapprove of this amendment, because it would open so wide a door for faction and intrigue, and afford such scope for the arts of an evil ambition. A man might go to the Senate with an incorruptible integrity, and the strongest attachment to the interest of his state. But if he deviated, in the least degree, from the line which a prevailing *party* in a popular assembly had marked for him, he would be immediately recalled. Under these circumstances, how easy would it be for an ambitious, factious demagogue to misrepresent him, to distort the features of his character, and give a false color to his conduct! How easy for such a man to impose upon the public, and influence them to recall and disgrace their faithful delegate! The general government may find it necessary to do many things which some states might never be willing to consent to. Suppose Congress should enter into a war to protect the fisheries, or any of the northern interests; the Southern States, loaded with their share of the burden which it would be necessary to impose, would condemn their representatives in the Senate for acquiescing in such a measure. There are a thousand things which an honest man might be obliged to do, from a conviction that it would be for the general good, which would give great dissatisfaction to his constituents.

Sir, all the arguments drawn from an imaginary prospect of corruption have little weight with me. From what source is this corruption to be derived? One gentleman tells you that this dreadful Senate is to be surrounded by a wall of adamant—of gold, and that this wall is to be a liquid one, and to flow in from all quarters. Such arguments as these seem rather the dreamings of a distempered fancy, than the cool, rational deductions of a deliberate mind. Whence is this corruption to be derived? Are the people to corrupt the senators with their own gold? Is *bribery* to enter the *federal city*, with the amazing influx of adamant the gentleman so pathetically contemplates? Are not Congress to publish, from time to time, an account of their receipts and expenditures [I.5.3]? Can there be any appropriation of money by the Senate, without the concurrence of the Assembly [I.1.1]? And can we suppose that a majority of both houses can be corrupted? At this rate we must suppose a miracle indeed.

But to return: The people are the best judges who ought to represent them. To dictate and control them, to tell them whom they shall not elect, is to abridge their natural rights. This rotation is an absurd species of ostracism—a mode of proscribing eminent merit, and banishing from stations of trust those who have filled them with the greatest faithfulness. Besides, it takes away the strongest stimulus to public virtue—the hope of honors and rewards. The acquisition of abilities is hardly worth the trouble, unless one is to enjoy the satisfaction of employing them for the good of one's country. We all know that experience is indispensably necessary to good government. Shall we, then, drive experience into obscurity? I repeat that this is an absolute abridgment of the people's rights.

As to the Senate's rendering themselves perpetual, or establishing such a power as to prevent their being removed, it appears to me chimerical. Can they make interest with their legislatures, who are themselves varying every year, sufficient for such a purpose? Can we suppose two senators will be able to corrupt the whole legislature of this state? The idea, I say, is chimerical. The thing is impossible.

JUNE 25

MR. SMITH resumed his argument, as follows: The amendment embraces two objects—first, that the senators shall be eligible for only six years in any term of twelve years; second, that they shall be subject to the recall of the legislatures of their several states. It is proper that we take up these points separately. I concur with the honorable gentleman[8] that there is a necessity for giving this branch a greater stability than the House of Representatives. I think his reasons are conclusive on this point. But, sir, it does not follow, from this position, that the *senators* ought to hold their places during life. Declaring them ineligible during a certain term after six years, is far from rendering them less stable than necessary. We think the amendments will place the Senate in a proper medium between a fluctuating and a perpetual body. As the clause now stands, there is no doubt that senators will hold their office perpetually; and in this situation they must of necessity lose their dependence, and attachments to the people. It is certainly inconsistent with the established principles of republicanism that the Senate should be a fixed and unchangeable body of men. There should be, then, some constitutional provision against this evil. A rotation I consider as the best possible mode of effecting a remedy. The amendment will not only have a tendency to defeat any plots which may be formed against the liberty and authority of the state governments, but will be the best means to extinguish the factions which often prevail, and which are sometimes so fatal to legislative bodies. This appears to me an important consideration. We have generally found that perpetual bodies have either combined in some scheme of usurpation, or have been torn and distracted with cabals. Both have been the source of misfortunes to the state. Most people acquainted with history will acknowledge these facts. Our Congress would have been a fine field for party spirit to act in. That body would undoubtedly have suffered all the evils of faction, had it not been secured by the rotation established by the Articles of Confederation. I think a *rotation* in the government is a very important and truly republican institution. All good republicans, I presume to say, will treat it with respect.

> Smith supposes that a senator eligible for reelection will have in effect a life tenure, and he offers rotation as a guard against a permanent Senate.

It is a circumstance strongly in favor of rotation, that it will have a tendency to diffuse a more general spirit of emulation, and to bring forward into office the genius and abilities of the continent: the ambition of gaining the qualifications necessary to govern will be in some proportion to the chance of success. If the office is to be perpetually confined to a few, other men, of equal talents and virtue, but not possessed of so extensive an influence, may

---

8. The gentleman is Hamilton, who the preceding day, June 24, argued for stability in the Senate.

be discouraged from aspiring to it. The more perfectly we are versed in the political science, the more firmly will the happy principles of republicanism be supported. The true policy of constitutions will be to increase the information of the country, and disseminate the knowledge of government as universally as possible. If this be done, we shall have, in any dangerous emergency, a numerous body of enlightened citizens, ready for the call of their country. As the Constitution now is, you only give an opportunity to two men to be acquainted with the public affairs. It is a maxim with me that every man employed in a high office by the people, should, from time to time, *return* to them, that he may be in a situation to satisfy them with respect to his conduct and the measures of administration. If I recollect right, it was observed by an honorable member from New York, that this amendment would be an infringement on the natural rights of the people. I humbly conceive, if the gentleman reflects maturely on the nature of his argument, he will acknowledge its weakness. What is government itself but a restraint upon the natural rights of the people? What constitution was ever devised that did not operate as a restraint on their original liberties? What is the whole system of qualifications, which take place in all free governments, but a restraint? Why is a certain age made necessary? why a certain term of citizenship? This Constitution itself, sir, has restraints innumerable. The amendment, it is true, may exclude two of the best men; but it can rarely happen that the state will sustain any material loss by this. I hope and believe that we shall always have more than two men who are capable of discharging the duty of a senator. But, if it should so happen that the state possessed only two capable men, it would be necessary they should return home, from time to time, to inspect and regulate our domestic affairs. I do not conceive the state can suffer any inconvenience. The argument, indeed, might have some weight, were the representation very large; but, as the power is to be exercised upon only two men, the apprehensions of the gentleman are entirely without foundation.

With respect to the second part of the amendment, I would observe, that, as the senators are the representatives of the *state legislatures*, it is reasonable and proper that they should be under their control. When a state sends an **agent** commissioned to transact any business, or perform any service, it certainly ought to have a power to recall. These are plain principles, and so far as they apply to the case under examination, they ought to be adopted by us. Form this government

Senators are **agents** of their states, in the view of Antifederalists.

as you please, you must, at all events, lodge in it very important powers. These powers must be in the hands of a few men, so situated as to procure a small degree of responsibility. These circumstances ought to put us upon our guard, and the inconvenience of this necessary delegation of power should be corrected, by providing some suitable checks.

Against this part of the amendment a great deal of argument has been used, and with considerable plausibility. It is said, if the amendment takes place, the senators will hold their office only during the pleasure of the state legislatures, and consequently will not possess the necessary firmness and stability. I conceive, sir, there is a fallacy in this argument, founded upon the suspicion that the legislature of a state will possess the qualities of a mob, and be incapable of any regular conduct. I know that the impulses of the multitude are inconsistent with systematic government. The people are frequently incompetent to deliberate discussion, and subject to errors and imprudences. Is this the complexion of the state legislatures? I presume it is not. I presume that they are never actuated by blind impulses; that they rarely do things hastily and without consideration. My apprehension is, that the power of recall would not be exercised as often as it ought. It is highly improbable that a man in whom the state has confided, and who has an established influence, will be recalled, unless his conduct has been notoriously wicked. The arguments of the gentleman, therefore, do not apply in this case. It is further observed, that it would be improper to give the legislatures this power, because the local interests and prejudices ought not to be admitted into the general government; and that, if the senator is rendered too dependent on his constituents, he will sacrifice the interests of the Union to the policy of his state. Sir, the Senate has been generally held up, by all parties, as a safeguard to the rights of the several states. In this view, the closest connection between them has been considered as necessary. But now, it seems, we speak in a different language; we now look upon the least attachment to their states as dangerous; we are now for separating them, and rendering them entirely independent, that we may root out the last vestige of state sovereignty. . . .

Another argument advanced by the gentlemen is, that our amendment would be the means of producing factions among the electors; *that aspiring men* would misrepresent the conduct of a faithful senator, and by intrigue procure a *recall upon false grounds*, in order to make room for themselves. But, sir, men who are ambitious for places will rarely be disposed to render those places unstable. A truly ambitious man will never do this, unless he is mad. It is not to be supposed that a state will recall a man once in twenty years, to make way for another. Dangers of this kind are very remote: I think they ought not to be brought seriously into view.

More than one of the gentlemen have ridiculed my apprehensions of corruption. How, say they, are the people to be corrupted? By their own money? Sir, in many countries, the people pay money to corrupt themselves: why should it not happen in this? Certainly, the Congress will be as liable to *corruption* as other bodies of men. Have they not the same frailties, and the same temptations? With respect to the corruption arising from the disposal of offices, the gentlemen have treated the argument as insignificant. But let any one make a calculation, and see whether there will not be good offices enough to dispose of to every man who goes there, who will then freely resign his seat; for can any one suppose that a member of Congress will not go out and relinquish his four dollars a day, for two or three thousand pounds a year? It is here objected that no man can hold an office created during the time he is in Congress [I.6.2]. But it will be easy for a man of influence, who has in his eye a favorite office previously created, and already filled, to say to his friend who holds it, Here, I will procure you another place of more emolument, provided you will relinquish yours in favor of me. The Constitution appears to be a restraint, when, in fact, it is none at all. I presume, sir, there is not a government in the world in which there is a greater scope for influence and corruption in the disposal of offices. Sir, I will not declaim, and say all men are dishonest; but I think, in forming a constitution, if we presume this, we shall be on the safest side. This extreme is certainly less dangerous than the other. It is wise to multiply checks to a greater degree than the present state of things requires. . . .

I have frequently observed a restraint upon the state governments, which Congress never can be under, construct that body as you please. It is a truth capable of demonstration, that the nearer the representative is to his constituents, the more attached and dependent he will be. In the states, the elections are frequent, and the representatives numerous: they transact business in the midst of their constituents, and every man must be called upon to account for his conduct. . . .

The Hon. Mr. HAMILTON. Mr. Chairman . . . There are two objects in forming systems of government—*safety* for the people, and *energy* in the administration. When these objects are united, the certain tendency of the system will be to the public welfare. If the latter object be neglected, the people's security will be as certainly sacrificed as by disregarding the former. Good constitutions are formed upon a comparison of the liberty of the individual with the strength of government: if the tone of either be too high, the other will be weakened too much. It is the happiest possible mode of conciliating these objects, to institute one branch peculiarly endowed with sensibility, another with knowledge and firmness. Through the opposition and mutual control of these bodies, the government will reach, in its operations, the perfect balance between liberty and power. The arguments of the gentlemen chiefly apply to the former branch—the House of Representatives. If they will calmly consider the different nature of the two branches, they will see that the reasoning which justly applies to the representative house, will go to destroy the essential qualities of the Senate. If the former is calculated perfectly upon the principles of caution, why should you impose the same principles upon the latter, which is designed for a different operation? Gentlemen, while they discover a laudable anxiety for the safety of the people, do not attend to the important distinction I have drawn. We have it constantly held up to us, that, as it is our chief duty to guard against tyranny, it is our policy to form all the branches of government for this purpose.

Sir, it is a truth sufficiently illustrated by experience, that when the *people* act by their representatives, they are commonly *irresistible*. The gentleman admits the position, that stability is essential to the government, and yet enforces principles which, if true, ought to banish stability from the system. The gentleman observes, that there is a fallacy in my reasoning, and informs us that the legislatures of the states, not the people, are to appoint the senators [I.3.1]. Does he reflect that they are the immediate agents of the people, that they are so constituted as to feel all their prejudices and passions, and to be governed, in a great degree, by their misapprehensions? Experience must have taught him the truth of this. Look through their history: what factions have arisen from the most trifling causes! What intrigues have been practiced for the most illiberal purposes! Is not the state of Rhode Island, at this moment, struggling under difficulties and distresses, for having been led blindly by the spirit of the multitude? What is her legislature but the picture of a *mob*? In this state, we have a senate, possessed of the proper qualities of a permanent body. Virginia, Maryland, and a few other states, are in the same situation. The rest are either governed by a single democratic assembly, or have a senate constituted entirely upon democratic principles. These have been more or less embroiled in factions, and have generally been the image and echo of the multitude.

It is difficult to reason on this point, without touching on certain delicate chords. I could refer you to periods and conjunctures when the people have been governed by improper passions, and led by factious and designing men.

Insofar as state legislatures, their senates included, reflect the passions of the populace, the chief purpose of the national Senate is to check the states, not represent them.

I could show that the same passions have infected their representatives. Let us beware that we do not make the state legislatures a vehicle in which the evil humors may be conveyed into the national system. To prevent this, it is necessary that the *Senate* should be so formed, as in some measure to check the *state governments*, and preclude the communication of the false impressions which they receive from the people. It has been often repeated, that the legislatures of the states can have only a partial and confined view of national affairs; that they can form no proper estimate of great objects which are not in the sphere of their interests. The observation of the gentleman, therefore, cannot take off the force of argument.

Sir, the senators will constantly be attended with a reflection, that their future existence is absolutely in the power of the states. Will not this form a powerful check? It is a reflection which applies closely to their feelings and interests; and no candid man, who thinks deliberately, will deny that it would be alone a sufficient check. The legislatures are to provide the mode of electing the President, and must have a great influence over the electors.[9] Indeed, they convey their influence, through a thousand channels, into the general government. Gentlemen have endeavored to show that there will be no clashing of local and general interests: they do not seem to have sufficiently considered the subject. We have, in this state, a duty of sixpence per pound on salt, and it operates lightly and with advantage; but such a duty would be very burdensome to some of the states. If Congress should, at any time, find it convenient to impose a salt tax, would it not be opposed by the Eastern States? Being themselves incapable of feeling the necessity of the measure, they could only feel its apparent injustice. Would it be wise to give the New England States a power to defeat this measure, by recalling their senators who may be engaged for it?

---

9. State legislatures determine the mode of election of their electors to the electoral college, the electing body of the president (II.1.2).

I beg the gentlemen once more to attend to the distinction between the real and the apparent interests of the states. I admit that the aggregate of individuals constitute the government; yet every state is not the government; every petty district is not the government. Sir, in our state legislatures, a *compromise* is frequently necessary between the interests of counties: the same must happen, in the general government, between states. In this, the few must yield to the many; or, in other words, the particular must be sacrificed to the general interest. If the members of Congress are too dependent on the state legislatures, they will be eternally forming secret combinations from local views. This is reasoning from the plainest principles. Their interest is interwoven with their dependence, and they will necessarily yield to the impression of their situation. Those who have been in Congress have seen these operations. The first question has been, How will such a measure affect my constituents, and, consequently, how will the part I take affect my re-election? This consideration may be in some degree proper; but to be dependent from day to day, and to have the idea perpetually present, would be the source of numerous evils. *Six years*, sir, is a period short enough for a proper degree of dependence.

Let us consider the peculiar state of this body, and see under what impressions they will act. *One third* of them are to go out at the end of two years, *two thirds* at four years, and the *whole* at six years [I.3.2]. When one year is elapsed, there is a number who are to hold their places for one year, others for three, and others for five years. Thus there will not only be a constant and frequent change of members, but there will be some whose office is near the point of expiration, and who, from this circumstance, will have a lively sense of their dependence. The *biennial* change of members is an excellent invention for increasing the difficulty of combination. Any scheme of usurpation will lose, every two years, a number of its oldest advocates, and their places will be supplied by an equal number of new, unaccommodating, and virtuous men.[10]

When two principles are equally important, we ought, if possible, to reconcile them, and sacrifice neither. We think that safety and permanency in this government are completely reconcilable. The state governments will have, from the causes I have described, a sufficient influence over the Senate, without the check for which the gentlemen contend [recall].

---

10. Hamilton expects turnover in the Senate, even with re-eligibility; Smith equates re-eligibility with permanency.

It has been remarked, that there is an inconsistency in our admitting that the *equal vote in the Senate* was given to secure the rights of the states, and at the same time holding up the idea that their interests should be sacrificed to those of the Union. But the committee certainly perceive the distinction between the rights of a state and its interests. The rights of a state are defined by the Constitution, and cannot be invaded without a violation of it; but the interests of a state have no connection with the Constitution, and may be, in a thousand instances, constitutionally sacrificed. A uniform tax is perfectly constitutional; and yet it may operate oppressively upon certain members of the Union. . . .

It is proper that the influence of the states should prevail to a certain extent. But shall the individual states be the judges how far? Shall an unlimited power be left them to determine in their own favor? The gentlemen go into the extreme: instead of a wise government, they would form a fantastical Utopia. But, sir, while they give it a plausible, popular shape, they would render it impracticable.

Much has been said about factions. As far as my observation has extended, factions in Congress have arisen from attachment to *state prejudices*. We are attempting, by this Constitution, to abolish factions, and to unite all parties for the general welfare.

That a man should have the power, in private life, of recalling his agent, is proper; because, in the business in which he is engaged, he has no other object but to gain the approbation of his principal. Is this the case with the senator? Is he simply the agent of the state? No. He is an **agent for the Union**, and he is bound to perform services necessary to the good of the whole, though his state should condemn them.

Senators are **agents for the Union**, trustees of the common good, in the view of Federalists.

Sir, in contending for a rotation, the gentlemen . . . deceive themselves; the amendment would defeat their own design. When a man knows he must quit his station, let his merit be what it may, he will turn his attention chiefly to his own emolument: nay, he will feel temptations, which few other situations furnish, to perpetuate his power by unconstitutional usurpations. Men will pursue their interests. It is as easy to change human nature as to oppose the strong current of the selfish passions. A wise legislator will gently divert the channel, and direct it, if possible, to the public good.

It has been observed, that it is not possible there should be in a state only two men qualified for senators. But, sir, the question is not, whether there may be no more than two men; but whether, in certain emergencies, you could find two equal to those whom the amendment would discard. Important negotiations, or other business to which they shall be most competent, may employ them at the moment of their removal. These things often happen. The difficulty of obtaining men capable of conducting the affairs of a nation in dangerous times, is much more serious than the gentlemen imagine

As to corruption, sir, admitting, in the *President*, a disposition to corrupt, what are the instruments of bribery? It is said he will have in his *disposal* a great number of *offices*. But how many offices are there, for which a man would relinquish the senatorial dignity? There may be some in the judicial, and some in other principal departments. But there are few whose respectability can, in any measure, balance that of the office of senator. Men who have been in the Senate once, and who have a reasonable hope of a re-election, will not be easily bought by offices. This reasoning shows that a *rotation* would be productive of many *disadvantages*: under particular circumstances, it might be extremely inconvenient, if not fatal to the prosperity of our country.

GORDON WOOD

FROM *The Creation of the American Republic, 1776–1787*

Historian Gordon Wood offers a social interpretation of the Constitution. Federalists were trying to preserve the aristocratic order of pre-Revolutionary America, while Antifederalists were trying to democratize society and government, argues Wood. Much of the debate was encapsulated in the parties' differing views of representation. As a historian, Wood is building an interpretation based on his reading of primary sources, some of which appear as Core Texts in the game book. Wood's interpretation is counted then as a secondary source.

Source: Gordon Wood, *The Creation of the American Republic, 1776–1787* (Chapel Hill: University of North Carolina Press, 1969), pp. 483–99, 506–18 (explanatory notes replace source citations by the author).

THOUGHT QUESTION: Can democratic egalitarianism recognize and accommodate aristocratic excellence? Can individuals achieve—wealth, power, distinction—without posing a threat to government by the people?

3. ARISTOCRACY AND DEMOCRACY

The division over the Constitution in 1787–88 is not easily analyzed. It is difficult, as historians have recently demonstrated, to equate the supporters or opponents of the Constitution with particular economic groupings. The Antifederalist politicians in the ratifying conventions often possessed wealth, including public securities, equal to that of the Federalists. While the relative youth of the Federalist leaders, compared to the ages of the prominent Antifederalists, was important, especially in accounting for the Federalists' ability to think freshly and creatively about politics, it can hardly be used to explain the division throughout the country. Moreover, the concern of the 1780's with America's moral character was not confined to the proponents of the Constitution. That rabid republican and Antifederalist, Benjamin Austin, was as convinced as any Federalist that "the luxurious living of all ranks and degrees" was "the principal cause of all the evils we now experience." Some leading Antifederalist intellectuals expressed as much fear of "the injustice, folly, and wickedness of the State Legislatures" and of "the usurpation and tyranny of the majority" against the minority as did Madison. In the Philadelphia Convention both [George] Mason and Elbridge Gerry, later prominent Antifederalists, admitted "the danger of the levelling spirit" flowing from "the excess of democracy" in the American republics. There were many diverse reasons in each state why men supported or opposed the Constitution that cut through any sort of class division. The Constitution was a single issue in a complicated situation, and its acceptance or rejection in many stares was often dictated by peculiar circumstances—the prevalence of Indians, the desire for western lands, the special interests of commerce—that defy generalization. Nevertheless, despite all of this confusion and complexity, the struggle over the Constitution, as the debate if nothing else makes clear, can best be understood as a social one. Whatever the particular constituency of the antagonists may have been, men in 1787–88 talked as if they were representing distinct and opposing social elements. Both the proponents and opponents of the Constitution focused throughout the debates on an essential point of political sociology that ultimately must be used to distinguish a Federalist from an Antifederalist. The quarrel was fundamentally one between aristocracy and democracy.

Because of its essentially social base, this quarrel, as George Minot of Massachusetts said, was "extremely unequal." To be sure, many Antifederalists, especially in Virginia, were as socially and intellectually formidable as any Federalist. Richard Henry Lee was undoubtedly the strongest mind the Antifederalists possessed, and he sympathized with the Antifederalist cause. Like Austin and other Antifederalists he believed that moral regeneration of America's character, rather than any legalistic manipulation of the constitutions of government, was the proper remedy for America's problems. "I fear," he wrote to George Mason in May 1787, "it is more in vicious manners, than mistakes in form, that we must seek for the causes of the present discontent." Still, such "aristocrats" as Lee or Mason did not truly represent Antifederalism. Not only did they reject the vicious state politics of the 1780's which Antifederalism, by the very purpose of the Constitution, was implicitly if not always explicitly committed to defend, but they could have no real identity, try as they might, with those for whom they sought to speak. Because, as Lee pointed out, "we must recollect how disproportionately the democratic and aristocratic parts of the community were represented" not only in the Philadelphia Convention but also in the ratifying conventions, many of the real Antifederalists, those intimately involved in the democratic politics of the 1780's and consequently with an emotional as well as an intellectual commitment to Antifederalism, were never clearly heard in the formal debates of 1787-88.

The disorganization and inertia of the Antifederalists, especially in contrast with the energy and effectiveness of the Federalists, has been repeatedly emphasized. The opponents of the Constitution lacked both coordination and unified leadership; "their principles," wrote Oliver Ellsworth, "are totally opposite to each other, and their objections discordant and irreconcilable." The Federalist victory, it appears, was actually more of an Antifederalist default. "We had no principle of concert or union," lamented the South Carolina Antifederalist, Aedanus Burke, while the supporters of the Constitution "left no expedient untried to push it forward." Madison's description of the Massachusetts Antifederalists was applicable to nearly all the states: "There was not a single character capable of uniting their wills or directing their measures. . . . They had no plan whatever. They looked no farther than to put a negative on the Constitution and return home." They were not, as one Federalist put it, "good politicians."

But the Antifederalists were not simply poorer politicians than the Federalists; they were actually different kinds of politicians. Too many of them were state-centered men with local interests and loyalties only, politicians without influence and connections, and ultimately politicians without social and intellectual confidence. In South Carolina the up-country opponents of the Constitution shied from debate and when they did occasionally rise to speak apologized effusively for their inability to say what they felt had to be said, thus leaving most of the opposition to the Constitution to be voiced by Rawlins Lowndes, a low-country planter who scarcely represented their interests and soon retired from the struggle. Elsewhere, in New Hampshire, Connecticut, Massachusetts, Pennsylvania, and North Carolina, the situation was similar: the Federalists had the bulk of talent and influence on their side "together with all the Speakers in the State great and small." In convention after convention the Antifederalists, as in Connecticut, tried to speak, but "they were browbeaten by many of those Cicero'es as they think themselves and others of Superior rank." "The presses are in a great measure secured to *their* side," the Antifederalists complained with justice: out of a hundred or more newspapers printed in the late eighties only a dozen supported the Antifederalists, as editors, "afraid to offend the great men, or Merchants, who could work their ruin," closed their columns to the opposition. The Antifederalists were not so much beaten as overawed. In Massachusetts the two leading socially established Antifederalists, Elbridge Gerry and James Warren, were defeated as delegates to the Ratifying Convention, and Antifederalist leadership consequently fell into the hands of newer, self-made men, of whom Samuel Nasson was perhaps typical—a Maine shopkeeper who was accused of delivering ghostwritten speeches in the Convention. Nasson had previously sat in the General Court but had declined reelection because he had been too keenly made aware of "the want of a proper Education I feel my Self So Small on many occasions that I all most Scrink into Nothing Besides I am often obliged to Borrow from Gentlemen that had advantages which I have not." Now, however, he had become the stoutest of Antifederalists, "full charged with Gass," one of those grumblers who, as Rufus King told Madison, were more afraid of the proponents of the Constitution than the Constitution itself, frightened that "some injury is plotted against them" because of "the extraordinary Union in favor of the Constitution in this State of the Wealthy and sensible part of it."

This fear of a plot by men who "talk so finely and gloss over matters so smoothly" ran through the Antifederalist mind. Because the many "new men" of the 1780's, men like Melancthon Smith and Abraham Yates of

New York or John Smilie and William Findley of Pennsylvania, had bypassed the social hierarchy in their rise to political leadership, they lacked those attributes of social distinction and dignity that went beyond mere wealth. Since these kinds of men were never assimilated to the gentlemanly cast of the Livingstons or the Morrises, they, like Americans earlier in confrontation with the British court, tended to view with suspicion and hostility the high-flying world of style and connections that they were barred by their language and tastes, if by nothing else, from sharing in. In the minds of these socially inferior politicians the movement for the strengthening of the central government could only be a "conspiracy" "planned and set to work" by a few aristocrats, who were at first, said Abraham Yates, no larger in number in any one state than the cabal which ought to undermine English liberty at the beginning of the eighteenth century. Since men like Yates could not quite comprehend what they were sure were the inner maneuverings of the elite, they were convinced that in the aristocrats' program, "what was their view in the beginning" or how "far it was Intended to be carried Must be Collected from facts that Afterwards have happened." Like American Whigs in the sixties and seventies forced to delve into the dark and complicated workings of English court politics, they could judge motives and plans "but by the Event." And they could only conclude that the events of the eighties, "the treasury, the Cincinnati,[1] and other public creditors, with all their concomitants," were "somehow or other, . . . inseparably connected," were all parts of a grand design "concerted by a few *tyrants*" to undo the Revolution and to establish an aristocracy in order "to lord it over the rest of their fellow citizens, to trample the poorer part of the people under their feet, that they may be rendered their servants and slaves." In this climate all the major issues of the Confederation period—the impost, commutation, and the return of the Loyalists—possessed a political and social significance that transcended economic concerns. All seemed to be devices by which a ruling few, like the ministers of the English Crown, would attach a corps of pensioners and dependents to the government and spread their influence and connections throughout the states in order "to dissolve our present Happy and Benevolent Constitution and to erect on the Ruins, a proper Aristocracy."

---

1. The Society of the Cincinnati was a confraternity of Revolutionary War officers. In the minds of some, including Thomas Jefferson, the Cincinnati represented a military junta threatening to the Republic.

Nothing was more characteristic of Antifederalist thinking than this obsession with aristocracy. Although to a European, American society may have appeared remarkably egalitarian, to many Americans, especially to those who aspired to places of consequence but were made to feel their inferiority in innumerable, often subtle, ways, American society was distinguished by its inequality. "It is true," said Melancthon Smith in the New York Ratifying Convention, "it is our singular felicity that we have no legal or hereditary distinctions . . .; but still there are real differences." "Every society naturally divides itself into classes . . . . Birth, education, talents, and wealth, create distinctions among men as visible, and of as much influence, as titles, stars, and garters." Everyone knew those "whom nature hath destined to rule," declared one sardonic Antifederalist pamphlet. Their "qualifications of authority" were obvious: "such as the dictatorial air, the magisterial voice, the imperious tone, the haughty countenance, the lofty look, the majestic mien." In all communities, "even in those of the most democratic kind," wrote George Clinton (whose "family and connections" in the minds of those like Philip Schuyler did not "entitle him to so distinguished a predominance" as the governorship of New York), there were pressures—"superior talents, fortunes and public employments"—demarcating an aristocracy whose influence was difficult to resist.

Such influence was difficult to resist because, to the continual annoyance of the Antifederalists, the great body of the people willingly submitted to it. The "authority of names" and "the influence of the great" among ordinary people were too evident to be denied. "Will any one say that there does not exist in this country the pride of family, of wealth, of talents, and that they do not command influence and respect among the common people?" "The people are too apt to yield an implicit assent to the opinions of those characters whose abilities are held in the highest esteem, and to those in whose integrity and patriotism they can confide; not considering that the love of domination is generally in proportion to talents, abilities and superior requirements." Because of this habit of deference in the people, it was "in the power of the enlightened and aspiring few, if they should combine, at any time to destroy the best establishments, and even make the people the instruments of their own subjugation." Hence, the Antifederalist-minded declared, the people must be awakened to the consequences of their self-ensnarement; they must be warned over and over by popular tribunes, by "those who are competent to the task of developing the principles of government," of the dangers involved in paying obeisance to those who they thought were their superiors. The people must "not be permitted to consider themselves as a grovelling, distinct species, uninterested in the general welfare."

Such constant admonitions to the people of the perils flowing from their too easy deference to the *"natural aristocracy"* were necessary because the Antifederalists were convinced that these "men that had been delicately bred, and who were in affluent circumstances," these "men of the most exalted rank in life," were by their very conspicuousness irreparably cut off from the great body of the people and hence could never share in its concerns nor look after its interests. It was not that these "certain men exalted above the rest" were necessarily "destitute of morality or virtue" or that they were inherently different from other men. "The same passions and prejudices govern all men." It was only that circumstances in their particular environment had made them different. There was "a charm in politicks"; men in high office become habituated with power, "grow fond of it, and are loath to resign it"; "they feel themselves flattered and elevated," enthralled by the attractions of high living, and thus they easily forget the interests of the common people, from which many of them once sprang. By dwelling so vividly on the allurements of prestige and power, by emphasizing again and again how the "human soul is affected by wealth, in all its faculties, . . . by its present interest, by its expectations, and by its fears," these ambitious Antifederalist politicians may have revealed as much about themselves as they did about the "aristocratic" elite they sought to displace. Yet at the same time by such language they contributed to a new appreciation of the nature of society.

The different lives led by the talented, the wealthy, and the powerful few—called the "natural aristocracy," in contrast to the conventional aristocracy of titled nobles—made them unsuitable representatives of ordinary people.

In these repeated attacks on deference and the capacity of a conspicuous few to speak for the whole society—which was to become in time the distinguishing feature of American democratic politics—the Antifederalists struck at the roots of the traditional conception of political society. If the natural elite, whether its distinctions were ascribed or acquired, was not in any organic way connected to the "feelings, circumstances, and interests" of the people and was incapable of feeling "sympathetically the wants of the people," then it followed that only ordinary men, men not distinguished by the characteristics of aristocratic wealth and taste, men "in middling circumstances" untempted by the attractions of a cosmopolitan world and thus "more temperate, of better morals, and less ambitious, than the great," could be trusted to speak for the great body of the people, for those who were coming more and more to be referred to as "the middling and lower classes of people." The differentiating influence of the environment was such that men in various ranks and classes now seemed to be broken apart from one another, separated by their peculiar circumstances into distinct,

Contrast with Burke's Speech to the Electors of Bristol.

unconnected, and often incompatible interests. With their indictment of aristocracy the Antifederalists were saying, whether they realized it or not, that the people of America even in their several states were not homogeneous entities each with a basic similarity of interest for which an empathic elite could speak. Society was not an organic hierarchy composed of ranks and degrees indissolubly linked one to another; rather it was a heterogeneous mixture of "many different classes or orders of people, Merchants, Farmers, Planter Mechanics and Gentry or wealthy Men." In such a society men from one class or group, however educated and respectable they may have been, could never be acquainted with the "*Situation* and Wants" of those of another class or group. Lawyers and planters could never be "adequate judges of tradesmens concerns." If men were truly to represent the people in government, it was not enough for them to be for the people; they had to be actually of the people. "Farmers, traders and mechanics . . . all ought to have a competent number of their best informed members in the legislature."

Thus the Antifederalists were not only directly challenging the conventional belief that only a gentlemanly few, even though now in America naturally and not artificially qualified, were best equipped through learning and experience to represent and to govern the society, but they were as well indirectly denying the assumption of organic social homogeneity on which republicanism rested. Without fully comprehending the consequences of their arguments the Antifederalists were destroying the great chain of being, thus undermining the social basis of republicanism and shattering that unity and harmony of social and political authority which the eighteenth century generally and indeed most Revolutionary leaders had considered essential to the maintenance of order.

By focusing on class division and the selfishness of the ruling elite, Antifederalists actually undermined republicanism, which rested on a conception of society as an organic and harmonious whole.

Confronted with such a fundamental challenge the Federalists initially backed away. They had no desire to argue the merits of the Constitution in terms of its social implications and were understandably reluctant to open up the character of American society as the central issue of the debate. But in the end they could not resist defending those beliefs in elitism that lay at the heart of their conception of politics and of their constitutional program. All of the Federalists' desires to establish a strong and respectable nation in the world, all of their plans to create a flourishing commercial economy, in short, all of what the Federalists wanted out of the new central government seemed in the final analysis dependent upon the prerequisite maintenance of aristocratic politics.

At first the Federalists tried to belittle the talk of an aristocracy; they even denied that they knew the meaning of the word. "Why bring into the debate the whims of writers—introducing the distinction of *well-born* from others?" asked Edmund Pendleton in the Virginia Ratifying Convention. In the Federalist view every man was *"well-born* who comes into the world with an intelligent mind, and with all his parts perfect." Was even natural talent to be suspect? Was learning to be encouraged, the Federalists asked in exasperation, only "to set up those who attained its benefits as butts of invidious distinction?" No American, the Federalists said, could justifiably oppose a man "commencing in life without any other stock but industry and economy," and "by the mere efforts of these" rising "to opulence and wealth." If social mobility were to be meaningful then some sorts of distinctions were necessary. If government by a natural aristocracy, said Wilson, meant "nothing more or less than a government of the best men in the community," then who could object to it? Could the Antifederalists actually intend to mark out those "most noted for their virtue and talents . . . as the most improper persons for the public confidence?" No, the Federalists exclaimed in disbelief, the Antifederalists could never have intended such a socially destructive conclusion. It was clear, said Hamilton, that the Antifederalists' arguments only proved "that there are men who are rich, men who are poor, some who are wise, and others who are not; that indeed, every distinguished man is an aristocrat."

But the Antifederalist intention and implication were too conspicuous to be avoided: all distinctions, whether naturally based or not, were being challenged. Robert Livingston in the New York Convention saw as clearly as anyone what he thought the Antifederalists were really after, and he minced no words in replying to Smith's attack on the natural aristocracy. Since Smith had classified as aristocrats not only "the rich and the great" but also "the wise, the learned, and those eminent for their talents or great virtues," aristocrats to the Antifederalists had in substance become all men of merit. Such men, such aristocrats, were not to be chosen for public office, questioned Livingston in rising disbelief in the implications of the Antifederalist argument, "because the people will not have confidence in them; that is, the people will not have confidence in those who best deserve and most possess their confidence?" The logic of Smith's reasoning, said Livingston, would lead to a government by the dregs of society, a monstrous government where all "the unjust, the selfish, the unsocial feelings," where all "the vices, the infirmities, the passions of the people" would be represented. "Can it be thought," asked Livingston in an earlier development of this argument to the Society of the Cincinnati, "that an enlightened people believe the science of government level to the meanest capacity? That experience, application, and education are unnecessary to those who are to frame laws for the government of the state?" Yet strange as it may have seemed to Livingston and others in the 1780's, America was actually approaching the point where ability, education, and wealth were becoming liabilities, not assets, in the attaining of public office." "Envy and the ambition of the unworthy" were robbing respectable men of the rank they merited. "To these causes," said Livingston, "we owe the cloud that obscures our internal governments."

The course of the debates over the Constitution seemed to confirm what the Federalists had believed all along. Antifederalism represented the climax of a "war" that was, in the words of Theodore Sedgwick, being "levied on the virtue, property, and distinctions in the community." The opponents of the Constitution, despite some, "particularly in Virginia," who were operating "from the most honorable and patriotic motives," were essentially identical with those who were responsible for the evils the states were suffering from in the eighties—"narrowminded politicians . . . under the influence of local views." "Whilst many *ostensible* reasons are assigned" for the Antifederalists' opposition, charged Washington, "the real ones are concealed behind the Curtains, because they are not of a nature to appear in open day." "The real object of all their zeal in opposing the system," agreed Madison, was to maintain "the supremacy of the State Legislatures," with all that meant in the printing of money and the violation of contracts. The Antifederalists or those for whom the Antifederalists spoke, whether their spokesmen realized it or not, were "none but the horse-jockey, the mushroom merchant, the running and dishonest speculator," those "who owe the most and have the least to pay," those "whose dependence and expectations are upon changes in government, and distracted times," men of "desperate Circumstances," those "in Every State" who "have Debts to pay, Interests to support or Fortunes to make," those, in short, who "wish· for scrambling Times." Apart from a few of their intellectual leaders the Antifederalists were thought to be an ill-bred lot: "Their education has been rather indifferent—they have been accustomed to think on the small scale." They were often blustering demagogues trying to push their way into office—"men of much self-importance and supposed skill in politics, who are not of sufficient consequence to obtain public employment." Hence they were considered to be jealous and mistrustful of "every one in the higher offices of society," unable to bear to see others possessing "that fancied blessing, to which, alas! they must themselves aspire in vain." In the Federalist mind therefore the struggle over the Constitution was not one between kinds of wealth or property, or one between commercial or noncommercial elements of the population, but rather represented a broad social division between those who believed in the right of a natural aristocracy to speak for the people and those who did not.

Against this threat from the licentious the Federalists pictured themselves as the defenders of the worthy, of those whom they called "the better sort of people," those, said John Jay, "who are orderly and industrious, who are content with their situations and not uneasy in their circumstances." Because the Federalists were fearful that republican equality was becoming "that *perfect equality* which deadens the motives of industry, and places Demerit on a Footing with Virtue," they were obsessed with the need to insure that the proper amount of inequality and natural distinctions be recognized. "Although there are no nobles in America," observed the French minister to America, Louis Otto, in 1786, "there is a class of men denominated 'gentlemen,' who, by reason of their wealth, their talents, their education, their families, or the offices they hold, aspire to a preeminence which the people refuse to grant them." "How idle . . . all disputes about a technical aristocracy" would be, if only the people would "pay strict attention to the natural aristocracy, which is the institution of heaven. . . . This aristocracy is derived from merit and that influence, which a character for superiour wisdom, and known services to the commonwealth, has to produce veneration, confidence and esteem, among a people, who have felt the benefits. . . ." Robert Morris, for example, was convinced there were social differences—even in Pennsylvania. "What! he exclaimed in scornful amazement at John Smilie's argument that a republic admitted of no social superiorities. "Is it insisted that there is no distinction of character?" Respectability, said Morris with conviction, was not confined to property. "Surely persons possessed of knowledge, judgment, information, integrity, and having extensive connections, are not to be classed with persons void of reputation or character."

In refuting the Antifederalists' contention "that all classes of citizens should have some of their own number in the representative body, in order that their feelings and interests may be the better understood and attended to," Hamilton in *The Federalist,* Number 35, put into words the Federalists' often unspoken and vaguely held assumption about the organic and the hierarchical nature of society. Such explicit class or occupational representation as the Antifederalists advocated, wrote Hamilton, was not only impractical but unnecessary, since the society was not as fragmented or heterogeneous as the Antifederalists implied. The various groups in the landed interest, for example, were "perfectly united, from the wealthiest landlord down to the poorest tenant," and this "common interest may always be reckoned upon as the surest bond of sympathy" linking the landed representative, however rich, to his constituents. In a like way, the members of the commercial community were "immediately connected" and most naturally represented by the merchants. "Mechanics and manufacturers will always be inclined, with few exceptions, to give their votes to merchants, in preference to persons of their own professions or trades. . . . They know that the merchant is their natural patron and friend; and . . . they are sensible that their habits in life have not been such as to give them those acquired endowments, without which in a deliberative assembly, the greatest natural abilities, are for the most part useless." However much many Federalists may have doubted the substance of Hamilton's analysis of American society, they could not doubt the truth of his conclusion. That the people were represented better by one of the natural aristocracy "whose situation leads to extensive inquiry and information" than by one "whose observation does not travel beyond the circle of his neighbors and acquaintances" was the defining element of the Federalist philosophy.

It was not simply the number of public securities, or credit outstanding, or the number of ships, or the amount of money possessed that made a man think of himself as one of the natural elite. It was much more subtle than the mere possession of wealth: it was a deeper social feeling, a sense of being socially established, of possessing attributes—family, education, and refinement—that others lacked, above all, of being accepted by and being able to move easily among those who considered themselves to be the respectable and cultivated. It is perhaps anachronistic to describe this social sense as a class interest, for it often transcended immediate political or economic concerns, and, as Hamilton's argument indicates, was designed to cut through narrow occupational categories. The Republicans of Philadelphia, for example, repeatedly denied that they represented an aristocracy with a united class interest. "We are of different occupations; of different sects of religion; and have different views of life. No factions or private system can comprehend us all." Yet with all their assertions of diversified interests the Republicans were not without a social consciousness in their quarrel with the supporters of the Pennsylvania Constitution.[2] If there were any of us ambitious for power, their apology continued, then there would be no need to change the Constitution, for we surely could attain power under the present Constitution. "We have already seen how easy the task is for *any character* to rise into power and consequence under it. And there are some of us, who think not so meanly of ourselves, as to dread any rivalship from those who are now in office."

In 1787 this kind of elitist social consciousness was brought into play as perhaps never before in eighteenth-century America, as gentlemen up and down the continent submerged their sectional and economic differences in the face of what seemed to be a threat to the very foundations of society. Despite his earlier opposition to the Order of the Cincinnati, Theodore Sedgwick, like other frightened New Englanders, now welcomed the organization as a source of strength in the battle for the Constitution. The fear of social disruption that had run through much of the writing of the eighties was brought to a head to eclipse all other fears. Although state politics in the

---

2. The Pennsylvania constitution of 1776 was the most democratic of all the states. Its opponents were sometimes called the Anti-Constitution Party and sometimes the Republican Party. They assumed control of state politics in time to elect delegates to the Constitutional Convention and to the state ratifying convention. Still in ascendance in 1790, they wrote a new constitution for Pennsylvania, one which, among other changes, gave the state a bicameral legislature.

eighties remains to be analyzed, the evidence from Federalist correspondence indicates clearly a belief that never had there occurred "so great a change in the opinion of the best people" as was occurring in the last few years of the decade. The Federalists were astonished at the outpouring in 1787 of influential and respectable people who had earlier remained quiescent. Too many of "the better sort of people," it was repeatedly said, had withdrawn at the end of the war "from the theatre of public action, to scenes of retirement and ease," and thus "demagogues of desperate fortunes, mere adventurers in fraud, were left to act unopposed." After all, it was explained, "when the wicked rise, men hide themselves." Even the problems of Massachusetts in 1786, noted General Benjamin Lincoln, the repressor of the Shaysites,[3] were not caused by the rebels, but by the laxity of "the good people of the state." But the lesson of this laxity was rapidly being learned. Everywhere, it seemed, men of virtue, good sense, and property, "almost the whole body of our enlighten'd and leading characters in every state," were awakened in support of stronger government. "The scum which was thrown upon the surface by the fermentation of the war is daily sinking," Benjamin Rush told Richard Price in 1786, "while a pure spirit is occupying its place." "Men are brought into action who had consigned themselves to an eve of rest," Edward Carrington wrote to Jefferson in June 1787, "and the Convention, as a Beacon, is rousing the attention of the Empire." The Antifederalists could only stand amazed at this "weight of talents" being gathered in support of the Constitution. "What must the individual be who could thus oppose them united?"

Still, in the face of this preponderance of wealth and respectability in support of the Constitution, what remains extraordinary about 1787–88 is not the weakness and disunity but the political strength of Antifederalism. That large numbers of Americans could actually reject a plan of government created by a body "compossd of the first characters in the Continent" and backed by Washington and nearly the whole of the natural aristocracy of the country said more about the changing character of American politics and society in the eighties than did the Constitution's eventual acceptance. It was indeed a portent of what was to come.

---

3. The reference is to Shays' Rebellion in Massachusetts during the winter of 1786–87.

5. THE FILTRATION OF TALENT

If the new national government was to promote the common good as force-
fully as any state government, and if, as the Federalists believed, a major
source of the vices of the eighties lay in the abuse of state power, then there
was something apparently contradictory about the new federal Constitution,
which after all represented not a weakening of the dangerous power of republican government but rather a strengthening of it. "The complaints against
the separate governments, even by the friends of the new plan," remarked the
Antifederalist James Winthrop, "are not that they have not power enough, but
that they are disposed to make a bad use of what power they have." Surely,
concluded Winthrop, the Federalists were reasoning badly "when they purpose to set up a government possess'd of much more extensive powers . . .
and subject to much smaller checks" than the existing state governments
possessed and were subject to. Madison for one was quite aware of the point-
edness of this objection. "It may be asked," he said, "how private rights will
be more secure under the Guardianship of the General Government than
under the State Governments, since they are both founded in the republican
principle which refers the ultimate decision to the will of the majority." What,
in other words, was different about the new federal Constitution that would
enable it to mitigate the effects of tyrannical majorities? What would keep
the new federal government from succumbing to the same pressures that
had beset the state governments? The answer the Federalists gave to these
questions unmistakably reveals the social bias underlying both their fears
of the unrestrained state legislatures and their expectations for their federal
remedy. For all of their desires to avoid intricate examination of a delicate
social structure, the Federalists' program itself demanded that the discussion
of the Constitution would be in essentially social terms.

The Federalists were not as much opposed to the governmental power of
the states as to the character of the people who were wielding it. The constitutions of most of the states were not really at fault. Massachusetts after all
possessed a nearly perfect constitution. What actually bothered the Federalists was the sort of people who had been able to gain positions of authority
in the state governments, particularly in the state legislatures. Much of the
quarrel with the viciousness, instability, and injustice of the various state
governments was at bottom social. "For, as John Dickinson emphasized,

"*the government will partake of the qualities of those whose authority is prevalent.*"
The political and social structures were intimately related. "People once
respected their governors, their senators, their judges and their clergy; they
reposed confidence in them; their laws were obeyed, and the states were
happy in tranquility." But in the eighties the authority of government had
drastically declined because "men of sense and property have lost much of
their influence by the popular spirit of the war." "That exact order, and due
subordination, that is essentially necessary in all well appointed governments, and which constitutes the real happiness and well being of society"
had been deranged by "men of no genius or abilities" who had tried to run
"the machine of government." Since "it cannot be expected that things will go
well, when persons of vicious principles, and loose morals are in authority,"
it was the large number of obscure, ignorant, and unruly men occupying the
state legislatures, and not the structure of the governments, that was the real
cause of the evils so much complained of.

The Federalist image of the Constitution as a sort of "philosopher's stone"
was indeed appropriate: it was a device intended to transmute base materials
into gold and thereby prolong the life of the republic. Patrick Henry acutely
perceived what the Federalists were driving at. "The Constitution," he said
in the Virginia Convention, "reflects in the most degrading and mortifying
manner on the virtue, integrity, and wisdom of the state legislatures; it pre-
supposes that the chosen few who go to Congress will have more upright
hearts, and more enlightened minds, than those who are members of the
individual legislatures." The new Constitution was structurally no different
from the constitutions of some of the states. Yet the powers of the new central
government were not as threatening as the powers of the state governments
precisely because the Federalists believed different kinds of persons would
hold them. They anticipated that somehow the new government would be
staffed largely by "the worthy," the natural social aristocracy of the country.
"After all," said Pelatiah Webster, putting his finger on the crux of the Federalist argument, "the grand secret of forming a good government, is, to put
good men into the administration: for wild, vicious, or idle men, will ever
make a bad government, let its principles be ever so good."

What was needed then, the Federalists argued, was to restore a proper
share of political influence to those who through their social attributes com-
manded the respect of the people and who through their enlightenment
and education knew the true policy of government. "The people commonly

intend the PUBLIC Good," wrote Hamilton in *The Federalist,* but they did not "always *reason right* about the *means* of promoting it." They sometimes erred, largely because they were continually beset "by the wiles of parasites and sycophants, by the snares of the ambitious, the avaricious, the desparate, by the artifices of men who possess their confidence more than deserve it, and of those who seek to possess rather than to deserve it." The rights of man were simple, quickly felt, and easily comprehended: in matters of liberty, "the mechanic and the philosopher, the farmer and the scholar, are all upon a footing." But to the Federalists matters of government were quite different: government was "a complicated science, and requires abilities and knowledge, of a variety of other subjects, to understand it." "Our states cannot be well governed," the Federalists concluded, "till our old influential characters acquire confidence and authority." Only if the respected and worthy lent their natural intellectual abilities and their natural social influence to political authority could governmental order be maintained.

Perhaps no one probed this theme more frenziedly than did Jonathan Jackson in his *Thoughts upon the Political Situation of the United States,* published in 1788. For Jackson the problems of the eighties were not merely intellectual but personal. Although at the close of the Revolution he had been one of the half-dozen richest residents of Newburyport, Massachusetts, by the end of the eighties not only had his wealth been greatly diminished but his position in Newburyport society had been usurped by a newer, less well-educated, less refined group of merchants. His pamphlet, expressing his bitter reaction to this displacement, exaggerated but did not misrepresent a common Federalist anxiety.

Although differences of rank were inevitable in every society, wrote Jackson, "there never was a people upon earth . . . who were in less hazard than the people of this country, of an aristocracy's prevailing—or anything like it, dangerous to liberty." America possessed very little "inequality of fortune." There was "no rank of any consequence, nor hereditary titles." "Landed property is in general held in small portions, even in southern states, compared with the manors, parks and royal demesnes of most countries." And the decay of primogeniture and entail,[4] together with the "diverse" habits and passions between fathers and sons, worked to retard the engrossing of large estates.

---

4. Primogeniture laws mandate that property descend intact to the firstborn son. Entail laws prohibit sale of property to persons not lineal descendants of the first owner. Both sets of laws aim at supporting a landed aristocracy.

The only kind of aristocracy possible in America would be an *"aristocracy* of experience, and of the best understandings," a *"natural aristocracy"* that had to dominate public authority in order to prevent America from degenerating into democratic licentiousness, into a government where the people "would be directed by no rule but their own will and caprice, or the interested wishes of a very few persons, who *affect* to speak the sentiments of the people." Tyranny by the people was the worst kind because it left few resources to the oppressed. Jackson explicitly and heatedly denied the assumption of 1776: "that large representative bodies are a great security to publick liberty." Such numerous popular assemblies resembled a mob, as likely filled with fools and knaves as wise and honest men. Jackson went on to question not only the possibility that the general good of the people would be expressed by such large assemblies, but also the advisability of annual elections and rotation of office. The people, Jackson even went so far as to say, "are nearly as unfit to choose legislators or any of the more important publick officers, as they are in general to fill the offices themselves." There were in fact too many examples in the eighties of men from the people gaining seats in America's public assemblies, men "of good natural abilities and sound understanding, but who had little or no education, and still less converse with the world." Such men were inevitably suspicious of those "they call the *gentle folks,"* those who were bred in easier circumstances and better endowed with education and worldly experience. Yet without the dominance of these "gentle folks" in the legislatures, the good of the whole society could never be promoted. The central problem facing America, said Jackson, was to bring the natural aristocracy back into use and to convey "authority to those, and those only, who by nature, education, and good dispositions, are qualified for government." It was this problem that the federal Constitution was designed to solve.

In a review of Jackson's pamphlet Noah Webster raised the crucial question. It was commendable, he wrote, that only the wise and honest men be elected to office. "But how can a constitution ensure the choice of such men? A constitution that leaves the choice entirely with the people?" It was not enough simply to state that such persons were to be chosen. Indeed, many of the state constitutions already declared "that senators and representatives *shall* be elected from the *most wise, able,* and *honest* citizens . . . . The truth is, such declarations are *empty things,* as they require *that* to be *done* which cannot be *defined,* much less *enforced."* It seemed to Webster that no constitution in a popular state could guarantee that only the natural aristocracy would be elected to office. How could the federal Constitution accomplish what the state constitutions like Massachusetts's and Connecticut's had been unable to accomplish? How could it insure that only the respectable and worthy would hold power?

The evils of state politics, the Federalists had become convinced, flowed from the narrowness of interest and vision of the state legislators. "We find the representatives of counties and corporations in the Legislatures of the States," said Madison, "much more disposed to sacrifice the aggregate interest, and even authority, to the local views of their Constituents" than to promote the general good at the expense of their electors. Small electoral districts enabled obscure and designing men to gain power by practicing "the vicious arts by which elections are too often carried." Already observers in the eighties had noticed that a governmental official "standing, not on local, but a general election of the whole body of the people" tended to have a superior, broader vision by "being the interested and natural conservator of the universal interest." "The most effectual remedy for the local biass" of senators or of any elected official, said Madison, was to impress upon their minds "an attention to the interest of the whole Society by making them the choice of the whole Society." If elected officials were concerned with only the interest of those who elected them, then their outlook was most easily broadened by enlarging their electorate. Perhaps nowhere was this contrast between localism and cosmopolitanism more fully analyzed and developed than in a pamphlet written by William Beers of Connecticut. Although Beers wrote in 1791, not to justify the Constitution, his insight into the workings of American politics was precisely that of the Federalists of 1787.

"The people of a state," wrote Beers, "may justly be divided into two classes": those, on one hand, "who are independent in their principles, of sound judgments, actuated by no local or personal influence, and who understand, and ever act with a view to the public good"; and those, on the other hand, who were "the dependent, the weak, the biassed, local party men—the dupes of artifice and ambition." While the independent and worthy were "actuated by a uniform spirit, and will generally unite their views in the same object," they were diffused throughout the whole community. "In particular districts, they bear not an equal proportion to the opposite party, who tho incapable of extending their views throughout the state, find in their particular communities similar objects of union." Thus the best people were often overpowered in small district elections, where "the success of a candidate may depend in a great degree on the quantity of his exertions for the moment," on his becoming "popular, for a single occasion, by qualities and means, which could not possibly establish a permanent popularity or one which should pervade a large community," on his seizing "the occasion of some prevailing passion, some strong impression of separate interest, some popular clamor against the existing administration, or some other false and fatal prejudice"—all the arts which were "well known, by the melancholy experience of this and other nations, to have met, in small circles of election, but too often with triumphant success." But an entire state could not be so deluded. "No momentary glare of deceptive qualities, no intrigues, no exertions will be sufficient to make a whole people lose sight of those points of character which alone can entitle one to their universal confidence." With a large electorate the advance toward public honors was slow and gradual. "Much time is necessary to become the object of general observation and confidence." Only established social leaders would thus be elected by a broad constituency. Narrow the electorate, "and you leave but a single step between the lowest and the most elevated station. You take ambition by the hand, you raise her from obscurity, and clothe her in purple."

The secret to securing representatives attentive to the common good is to have them elected by the whole community, or to enlarge the size of electoral districts while reducing the size of the legislative body.

With respect to the size of the legislative body, the converse was true. Reduce the number of its members and thereby guarantee a larger proportion of the right kind of people to be elected, for "the more you enlarge the body, the greater chance there is, of introducing weak and unqualified men."

Constitutional reformers in the eighties had continually attempted to apply these insights to the states, by decreasing the size of the legislatures and by proposing at-large elections for governors and senators in order to "make a segregation of upright, virtuous, intelligent men, to guide the helm of public affairs." Now these ideas were to be applied to the new federal government with hopefully even more effectiveness. The great height of the new national government, it was expected, would prevent unprincipled and vicious men, the obscure and local-minded men who had gained power in the state legislatures, from scaling its walls. The federal government would act as a kind of sieve, extracting "from the mass of the society the purest and noblest characters which it contains." Election by the people in large districts would temper demagoguery and crass electioneering and would thus, said James Wilson, "be most likely to obtain men of intelligence and uprightness." "Faction," it was believed, "will decrease in proportion to the diminution of counsellors." It would be "transferred from the state legislatures to Congress, where it will be more easily controlled." The men who would sit in the federal legislature, because few in number and drawn from a broad electorate, would be "the best men in the country." "For," wrote John Jay in *The Federalist*, "although town or county, or other contracted influence, may place men in State assemblies, or senates, or courts of justice, or executive departments, yet more general and extensive reputation for talents and other qualifications will be necessary to recommend men to offices under the national government." Only by first bringing these sorts of men, the natural aristocracy of the country, back into dominance in politics, the Federalists were convinced, could Americans begin to solve the pressing foreign and domestic problems facing them. Only then, concluded Jay, would it "result that the administration, the political counsels, and the judicial decisions of the national government will be more wise, systematical, and judicious than those of individual States, and consequently more satisfactory with respect to other nations, as well as more *safe* with respect to us." The key therefore to the prospects of the new federal government, compared to the experience of the confederation of sovereign states, declared Francis Corbin of Virginia in words borrowed from Jean Louis De Lolme, the Genevan commentator on the English constitution, lay in the fact that the federal Constitution "places the remedy in the hands which *feel* the disorder; the other places the remedy in those hands which *cause* the disorder."

In short, through the artificial contrivance of the Constitution overlying an expanded society, the Federalists meant to restore and to prolong the traditional kind of elitist influence in politics that social developments, especially since the Revolution, were undermining. As the defenders if not always the perpetrators of these developments—the "disorder" of the 1780's—the Antifederalists could scarcely have missed the social implications of the Federalist program. The Constitution was intrinsically an aristocratic document designed to check the democratic tendencies of the period, and as such it dictated the character of the Antifederalist response.

> Here Wood states his thesis—that the Constitution is an aristocratic document—if only as seen by the Antifederalists.

It was therefore inevitable that the Antifederalists should have charged that the new government was "dangerously adapted to the purposes of an immediate *aristocratic tyranny.*" In state after state the Antifederalists reduced the issue to those social terms predetermined by the Federalists themselves: the Constitution was a plan intended to "raise the fortunes and respectability of the *well-born few,* and oppress the plebians"; it was "a continental exertion of the *well-born* of America to obtain that darling domination, which they have not been able to accomplish in their respective states"; it "will lead to an aristocratical government, and establish tyranny over us." Whatever their own particular social standing, the Antifederalist spokesmen spread the warning that the new government either would be "in practice a *permanent* ARISTOCRACY" or would soon "degenerate to a compleat Aristocracy." Both George Mason and Richard Henry Lee, speaking not out of the concerns of the social elite to which they belonged but out of a complicated sense of alienation from that elite, expressed as much fear of a "consolidating aristocracy" resulting from the new Constitution as any uncultivated Scotch-Irish upstart. While Lee privately revealed his deep dislike of "the hasty, unpersevering, aristocratic genius of the south" which "suits not my disposition," Mason throughout the duration of the Philadelphia Convention acted as the conscience of an old republicanism he thought his Virginia colleagues had forgotten and continually reminded them of what the Revolution had been about. "Whatever inconveniency may attend the democratic principle," said Mason repeatedly, "it must actuate one part of the Government. It is the only security for the rights of the people." As the Constitution seemed to demonstrate, the "superior classes of society" were becoming too indifferent to the "lowest classes." Remember, he warned his fellow delegates pointedly, "our own children will in a short time be among the general mass." The Constitution seemed obviously "calculated," as even young John Quincy Adams declared, "to increase the influence, power and wealth of those who have it already." Its adoption would undoubtedly be "a grand point gained in favor of the aristocratic party."

Aristocratic principles were in fact "interwoven" in the very fabric of the proposed government. If a government was "so constituted as to admit but few to exercise the powers of it," then it would "according to the natural course of things" end up in the hands of "the natural aristocracy." It went almost without saying that the awesome president and the exalted Senate, "a compound of *monarchy* and *aristocracy*," would be dangerously far removed from the people. But even the House of Representatives, the very body that "should be a true picture of the people, possess a knowledge of their circumstances and their wants, sympathize in all their distresses, and disposed to seek their true interest was without "a tincture of democracy." Since it could never collect "the interests, feelings, and opinions of three or four millions of people," it was better understood as "an Assistant Aristocratical Branch" to the Senate than as a real representation of the people. When the number of representatives was "so small, the office will be highly elevated and distinguished; the style in which the members live will probably be high; circumstances of this kind will render the place of a representative not a desirable one to sensible substantial men, who have been used to walk in the plain and frugal paths of life." While the ordinary people in extensive electoral districts of thirty or forty thousand inhabitants would remain "divided," those few extraordinary men with "conspicuous military, popular, civil or legal talents" could more easily form broader associations to dominate elections; they had family and other connections to "unite their interests." If only a half-dozen congressmen were to be selected to represent a large state, then rarely, argued the Antifederalists in terms that were essentially no different "from those used by the Federalists in the Constitution's defense, would persons from "the great body of the people, the middle and lower classes," be elected to the House of Representatives. "The Station is too high and exalted to be filled but [by] the *first Men* in the State in point of Fortune and Influence. In fact no order or class of the people will be represented in the House of Representatives called the Democratic Branch but the rich and wealthy." The Antifederalists thus came to oppose the new national government for the same reason the Federalists favored it: because its very structure and detachment from the people would work to exclude any kind of actual and local interest representation and prevent those who were not rich, well born, or prominent from exercising political power. Both sides fully appreciated the central issue the Constitution posed and grappled with it throughout the debates: whether a professedly popular government should actually be in the hands of, rather than simply derived from, common ordinary people.

Federalists and Antifederalists agreed that the Constitution was designed to keep the public at some remove from the exercise of power. They disagreed on their appreciation of that fact.

Out of the division in 1787–88 over this issue, an issue which was as conspicuously social as any in American history, the Antifederalists emerged as the spokesmen for the growing American antagonism to aristocracy and as the defenders of the most intimate participation in politics of the widest variety of people possible. It was not from lack of vision that the Antifederalists feared the new government. Although their viewpoint was intensely localistic, it was grounded in as perceptive an understanding of the social basis of American politics as that of the Federalists. Most of the Antifederalists were majoritarians with respect to the state legislatures but not with respect to the national legislature, because they presumed as well as the Federalists did that different sorts of people from those who sat in the state assemblies would occupy the Congress. Whatever else may be said about the Antifederalists, their populism cannot be impugned. They were true champions of the most extreme kind of democratic and egalitarian politics expressed in the Revolutionary era. Convinced that "it has been the principal care of free governments to guard against the encroachments of the great," the Antifederalists believed that popular government itself, as defined by the principles of 1776, was endangered by the new national government. If the Revolution had been a transfer of power from the few to the many, then the federal Constitution clearly represented an abnegation of the Revolution.

Here's the corollary to Wood's thesis—the Constitution was an abnegation of the Revolution.

For, as Richard Henry Lee wrote in his *Letters from the Federal Farmer,* "every man of reflection must see, that the change now proposed, is a transfer of power from the many to the few."

Although Lee's analysis contained the essential truth, the Federalist program was not quite so simply summed up. It was true that through the new Constitution the Federalists hoped to resist and eventually to avert what they saw to be the rapid decline of the influence and authority of the natural aristocracy in America. At the very time that the organic conception of society that made elite rule comprehensible was finally and avowedly dissolving, and the members of the elite were developing distinct professional, social, or economic interests, the Federalists found elite rule more imperative than ever before. To the Federalists the greatest dangers to republicanism were flowing not, as the old Whigs had thought, from the rulers or from any distinctive minority in the community, but from the widespread participation of the people in the government. It now seemed increasingly evident that if the public good not only of the United States as a whole but even of the separate states were to be truly perceived and promoted, the American people must abandon their Revolutionary reliance on their representative state legislatures and place their confidence in the highmindedness of the natural leaders of the society, which ideally everyone had the opportunity of becoming. Since the Federalists presumed that only such a self-conscious elite could transcend the many narrow and contradictory interests inevitable in any society, however small, the measure of a good government became its capacity for insuring the predominance of these kinds of natural leaders who knew better than the people as a whole what was good for the society.

The result was an amazing display of confidence in constitutionalism, in the efficacy of institutional devices for solving social and political problems. Through the proper arrangement of new institutional structures the Federalists aimed to turn the political and social developments that were weakening the place of "the better sort of people" in government back upon themselves and to make these developments the very source of the perpetuation of the natural aristocracy's dominance of politics. Thus the Federalists did not directly reject democratic politics as it had manifested itself in the 1780's; rather they attempted to adjust to this politics in order to control and mitigate its effects. In short they offered the country an elitist theory of democracy. They did not see themselves as repudiating either the Revolution or popular government, but saw themselves as saving both from their excesses. If the Constitution were not established, they told themselves and the country over and over, then republicanism was doomed, the grand experiment was over, and a division of the confederacy, monarchy, or worse would result.

> Here, finally, is the Federalist reply—not subverting democracy but saving democracy from its worst excesses.

Despite all the examples of popular vice in the eighties, the Federalist confidence in the people remained strong. The letters of "Caesar," with their frank and violent denigration of the people, were anomalies in the Federalist literature. The Federalists had by no means lost faith in the people, at least in the people's ability to discern their true leaders. In fact many of the social elite who comprised the Federalist leadership were confident of popular election if the constituency could be made broad enough, and crass electioneering be curbed, so that the people's choice would be undisturbed by ambitious demagogues. "For if not blind to their own interest, they choose men of the first character for wisdom and integrity." Despite prodding by so-called designing and unprincipled men, the bulk of the people remained deferential to the established social leadership—for some aspiring politicians frustratingly so.

Even if they had wanted to, the Federalists could not turn their backs on republicanism. For it was evident to even the most pessimistic "that no other form would be reconcilable with the genius of the people of America; with the fundamental principles of the Revolution; or with that honorable determination which animates every votary of freedom, to rest all our political experiments on the capacity of mankind for self-government." Whatever government the Federalists established had to be "strictly republican" and "deducible from the only source of just authority—the People."

Appendix: Constitution of the United States

We the People of the United States, in order to form a more perfect Union, establish justice, insure domestic tranquility, provide for the common defense, promote the general welfare, and secure the blessings of liberty to ourselves and our posterity, do ordain and establish this Constitution for the United States of America.

Article I.

Section. 1.

All legislative Powers herein granted shall be vested in a Congress of the United States, which shall consist of a Senate and House of Representatives.

Section. 2.

The House of Representatives shall be composed of members chosen every second year by the people of the several States, and the electors in each State shall have the qualifications requisite for electors of the most numerous branch of the State legislature.

No person shall be a representative who shall not have attained to the age of twenty-five years, and been seven years a citizen of the United States, and who shall not, when elected, be an inhabitant of that State in which he shall be chosen.

Representatives and direct taxes shall be apportioned among the several States which may be included within this Union, according to their respective numbers, which shall be determined by adding to the whole number of free persons, including those bound to service for a term of years, and excluding Indians not taxed, three-fifths of all other persons. The actual enumeration shall be made within three years after the first meeting of the Congress of the United States, and within every subsequent term of ten years, in such manner as they shall by law direct. The number of representatives shall not exceed one for every thirty thousand, but each State shall have at least one representative; and until such enumeration shall be made, the State of New Hampshire shall be entitled to choose three, Massachusetts eight, Rhode-Island and Providence Plantations one, Connecticut five, New-York six, New Jersey four, Pennsylvania eight, Delaware one, Maryland six, Virginia ten, North Carolina five, South Carolina five, and Georgia three.

When vacancies happen in the representation from any State, the executive authority thereof shall issue writs of election to fill such vacancies.

The House of Representatives shall choose their Speaker and other officers; and shall have the sole power of impeachment.

Section. 3.

The Senate of the United States shall be composed of two senators from each State, chosen by the legislature thereof, for six years; and each senator shall have one vote.

Immediately after they shall be assembled in consequence of the first election, they shall be divided as equally as may be into three classes. The seats of the senators of the first class shall be vacated at the expiration of the second year, of the second class at the expiration of the fourth year, and of the third class at the expiration of the sixth year, so that one third may be chosen every second year; and if vacancies happen by resignation, or otherwise, during the recess of the legislature of any State, the executive thereof may make temporary appointments until the next meeting of the legislature, which shall then fill such vacancies.

No person shall be a senator who shall not have attained to the age of thirty years, and been nine years a citizen of the United States, and who shall not, when elected, be an inhabitant of that State for which he shall be chosen.

The Vice President of the United States shall be President of the Senate, but shall have no vote, unless they be equally divided.

The Senate shall choose their other officers, and also a president pro tempore, in the absence of the Vice President, or when he shall exercise the office of President of the United States.

The Senate shall have the sole power to try all impeachments. When sitting for that purpose, they shall be on oath or affirmation. When the President of the United States is tried, the Chief Justice shall preside. And no person shall be convicted without the concurrence of two-thirds of the members present.

Judgment in cases of impeachment shall not extend further than to removal from office, and disqualification to hold and enjoy any office of honor, trust or profit under the United States; but the party convicted shall nevertheless be liable and subject to indictment, trial, judgment and punishment, according to law.

Section. 4.

The times, places and manner of holding elections for senators and representatives, shall be prescribed in each State by the legislature thereof; but the Congress may at any time by law make or alter such regulations, except as to the places of choosing senators.

The Congress shall assemble at least once in every year, and such meeting shall be on the first Monday in December, unless they shall by law appoint a different day.

Section. 5.

Each house shall be the judge of the elections, returns and qualifications of its own members, and a majority of each shall constitute a quorum to do business; but a smaller number may adjourn from day to day, and may be authorized to compel the attendance of absent members, in such manner, and under such penalties as each house may provide.

Each house may determine the rules of its proceedings, punish its members for disorderly behavior, and, with the concurrence of two-thirds, expel a member.

Each house shall keep a journal of its proceedings, and from time to time publish the same, excepting such parts as may in their judgment require secrecy; and the yeas and nays of the members of either house on any question shall, at the desire of one-fifth of those present, be entered on the journal.

Neither house, during the session of Congress, shall, without the consent of the other, adjourn for more than three days, nor to any other place than that in which the two houses shall be sitting.

Section. 6.

The senators and representatives shall receive a compensation for their services, to be ascertained by law, and paid out of the treasury of the United States. They shall in all cases, except treason, felony and breach of the peace, be privileged from arrest during their attendance at the session of their respective houses, and in going to and returning from the same; and for any speech or debate in either house, they shall not be questioned in any other place.

No senator or representative shall, during the time for which he was elected, be appointed to any civil office under the authority of the United States, which shall have been created, or the emoluments whereof shall have been increased during such time; and no person holding any office under the United States, shall be a member of either house during his continuance in office.

Section. 7.

All bills for raising revenue shall originate in the House of Representatives; but the Senate may propose or concur with amendments as on other bills.

Every bill which shall have passed the House of Representatives and the Senate, shall, before it become a law, be presented to the President of the United States; if he approve he shall sign it, but if not he shall return it, with his objections to that house in which it shall have originated, who shall enter the objections at large on their journal, and proceed to reconsider it. If after such reconsideration two thirds of that house shall agree to pass the bill, it shall be sent, together with the objections, to the other house, by which it shall likewise be reconsidered, and if approved by two-thirds of that house, it shall become a law. But in all such cases the votes of both houses shall be determined by yeas and nays, and the names of the persons voting for and against the bill shall be entered on the journal of each house respectively. If any bill shall not be returned by the President within ten days (Sundays excepted) after it shall have been presented to him, the same shall be a law, in like manner as if he had signed it, unless the Congress by their adjournment prevent its return, in which case it shall not be a law.

Every order, resolution, or vote to which the concurrence of the Senate and House of Representatives may be necessary (except on a question of adjournment) shall be presented to the President of the United States; and before the same shall take effect, shall be approved by him, or being disapproved by him, shall be repassed by two-thirds of the Senate and House of Representatives, according to the rules and limitations prescribed in the case of a bill.

Section. 8.

The Congress shall have power to lay and collect taxes, duties, imposts and excises, to pay the debts and provide for the common defense and general welfare of the United States; but all duties, imposts and excises shall be uniform throughout the United States;

To borrow money on the credit of the United States;

To regulate commerce with foreign nations, and among the several States, and with the Indian tribes;

To establish an uniform rule of naturalization, and uniform laws on the subject of bankruptcies throughout the United States;

To coin money, regulate the value thereof, and of foreign coin, and fix the standard of weights and measures;

To provide for the punishment of counterfeiting the securities and current coin of the United States;

To establish post offices and post roads;

To promote the progress of science and useful arts, by securing for limited times to authors and inventors the exclusive right to their respective writings and discoveries;

To constitute tribunals inferior to the Supreme Court;

To define and punish piracies and felonies committed on the high seas, and offenses against the law of nations;

To declare war, grant letters of marque and reprisal, and make rules concerning captures on land and water;

To raise and support armies, but no appropriation of money to that use shall be for a longer term than two years;

To provide and maintain a navy;

To make rules for the government and regulation of the land and naval forces;

To provide for calling forth the militia to execute the laws of the union, suppress insurrections and repel invasions;

To provide for organizing, arming, and disciplining, the militia, and for governing such part of them as may be employed in the service of the United States, reserving to the States respectively, the appointment of the officers, and the authority of training the militia according to the discipline prescribed by Congress;

To exercise exclusive legislation in all cases whatsoever, over such district (not exceeding ten miles square) as may, by cession of particular States, and the acceptance of Congress, become the seat of the government of the United States, and to exercise like authority over all places purchased by the consent of the legislature of the State in which the same shall be, for the erection of forts, magazines, arsenals, dock-yards, and other needful buildings; And

To make all laws which shall be necessary and proper for carrying into execution the foregoing powers, and all other powers vested by this Constitution in the government of the United States, or in any department or officer thereof.

Section. 9.

The migration or importation of such persons as any of the States now existing shall think proper to admit, shall not be prohibited by the Congress prior to the year one thousand eight hundred and eight, but a tax or duty may be imposed on such importation, not exceeding ten dollars for each person.

The privilege of the writ of habeas corpus shall not be suspended, unless when in cases of rebellion or invasion the public safety may require it.

No bill of attainder or ex post facto law shall be passed.

No capitation, or other direct, tax shall be laid, unless in proportion to the census or enumeration herein before directed to be taken.

No preference shall be given by any regulation of commerce or revenue to the ports of one State over those of another; nor shall vessels bound to, or from, one State, be obliged to enter, clear, or pay duties in another.

No money shall be drawn from the treasury, but in consequence of appropriations made by law; and a regular statement and account of the receipts and expenditures of all public money shall be published from time to time.

No title of nobility shall be granted by the United States: And no person holding any office of profit or trust under them, shall, without the consent of the Congress, accept of any present, emolument, office, or title, of any kind whatever, from any king, prince, or foreign state.

Section. 10.

No State shall enter into any treaty, alliance, or confederation; grant letters of marque and reprisal; coin money; emit bills of credit; make any thing but gold and silver coin a tender in payment of debts; pass any bill of attainder, ex post facto law, or law impairing the obligation of contracts, or grant any title of nobility.

No State shall, without the consent of the Congress, lay any imposts or duties on imports or exports, except what may be absolutely necessary for executing its inspection laws; and the net produce of all duties and imposts, laid by any State on imports or exports, shall be for the use of the treasury of the United States; and all such laws shall be subject to the revision and control of the Congress.

No State shall, without the consent of Congress, lay any duty of tonnage, keep troops, or ships of war in time of peace, enter into any agreement or compact with another State, or with a foreign power, or engage in war, unless actually invaded, or in such imminent danger as will not admit of delay.

Article II.

Section. 1.

The executive power shall be vested in a President of the United States of America. He shall hold his office during the term of four years, and, together with the Vice President, chosen for the same term, be elected, as follows:

Each State shall appoint, in such manner as the legislature thereof may direct, a number of electors, equal to the whole number of senators and representatives to which the State may be entitled in the Congress: but no senator or representative, or person holding an office of trust or profit under the United States, shall be appointed an elector.

The electors shall meet in their respective States, and vote by ballot for two persons, of whom one at least shall not be an inhabitant of the same State with themselves. And they shall make a list of all the persons voted for, and the number of votes for each; which list they shall sign and certify, and transmit sealed to the seat of the government of the United States, directed to the president of the Senate. The president of the Senate shall, in the presence of the Senate and House of Representatives, open all the certificates, and the votes shall then be counted. The person having the greatest number of votes shall be the President, if such number be a majority of the whole number of electors appointed; and if there be more than one who have such majority, and have an equal number of votes, then the House of Representatives shall immediately choose by ballot one of them for President; and if no person have a majority, then from the five highest on the list the said House shall in like manner choose the President. But in choosing the President, the votes shall be taken by States, the representation from each State having one vote; a quorum for this purpose shall consist of a member or members from two-thirds of the States, and a majority of all the States shall be necessary to a choice. In every case, after the choice of the President, the person having the greatest number of the electors shall be the Vice-President. But if there should remain two or more who have equal votes, the Senate shall choose from them by ballot the Vice-President.

The Congress may determine the time of choosing the electors, and the day on which they shall give their votes; which day shall be the same throughout the United States.

No person except a natural-born citizen, or a citizen of the United States, at the time of the adoption of this Constitution, shall be eligible to the office of President; neither shall any person be eligible to that office who shall not have attained to the age of thirty-five years, and been fourteen years a resident within the United States.

In case of the removal of the President from office, or of his death, resignation, or inability to discharge the powers and duties of the said office, the same shall devolve on the Vice-President, and the Congress may by law provide for the case of removal, death, resignation, or inability, both of the President and Vice-President, declaring what officer shall then act as President, and such officer shall act accordingly, until the disability be removed, or a President shall be elected.

The President shall, at stated times, receive for his services, a compensation, which shall neither be increased nor diminished during the period for which he shall have been elected, and he shall not receive within that period any other emolument from the United States, or any of them.

Before he enter on the execution of his office, he shall take the following oath or affirmation: "I do solemnly swear (or affirm) that I will faithfully execute the office of President of the United States, and will to the best of my ability, preserve, protect and defend the Constitution of the United States."

Section. 2.

The President shall be commander-in-chief of the army and navy of the United States, and of the militia of the several States, when called into the actual service of the United States; he may require the opinion, in writing, of the principal officer in each of the executive departments, upon any subject relating to the duties of their respective offices, and he shall have power to grant reprieves and pardons for offenses against the United States, except in cases of impeachment.

He shall have power, by and with the advice and consent of the Senate, to make treaties, provided two-thirds of the senators present concur; and he shall nominate, and by and with the advice and consent of the Senate, shall appoint ambassadors, other public ministers and consuls, judges of the Supreme Court, and all other officers of the United States, whose appointments are not herein otherwise provided for, and which shall be established by law. But the Congress may by law vest the appointment of such inferior officers, as they think proper, in the President alone, in the courts of law, or in the heads of departments.

The President shall have power to fill up all vacancies that may happen during the recess of the Senate, by granting commissions which shall expire at the end of their next session.

Section. 3.

He shall from time to time give to the Congress information of the state of the Union, and recommend to their consideration such measures as he shall judge necessary and expedient; he may, on extraordinary occasions, convene both houses, or either of them, and in case of disagreement between them, with respect to the time of adjournment, he may adjourn them to such time as he shall think proper; he shall receive ambassadors and other public ministers; he shall take care that the laws be faithfully executed, and shall commission all the officers of the United States.

Section. 4.

The President, Vice President and all civil officers of the United States, shall be removed from office on impeachment for, and conviction of, treason, bribery, or other high crimes and misdemeanors.

Article III.

Section. 1.

The judicial Power of the United States shall be vested in one Supreme Court, and in such inferior courts as the Congress may from time to time ordain and establish. The judges, both of the supreme and inferior courts, shall hold their offices during good behavior, and shall, at stated times, receive for their services a compensation, which shall not be diminished during their continuance in office.

Section. 2.

The judicial power shall extend to all cases, in law and equity, arising under this Constitution, the laws of the United States, and treaties made, or which shall be made, under their authority; to all cases affecting ambassadors, other public ministers and consuls; to all cases of admiralty and maritime jurisdiction; to controversies to which the United States shall be a party; to controversies between two or more States; between a State and citizens of another State, between citizens of different States, between citizens of the same State claiming lands under grants of different States, and between a State, or the citizens thereof, and foreign states, citizens or subjects.

In all cases affecting ambassadors, other public ministers and consuls, and those in which a State shall be party, the Supreme Court shall have original jurisdiction. In all the other cases before mentioned, the Supreme Court shall have appellate jurisdiction, both as to law and fact, with such exceptions, and under such regulations as the Congress shall make.

The trial of all crimes, except in cases of impeachment, shall be by jury; and such trial shall be held in the State where the said crimes shall have been committed; but when not committed within any State, the trial shall be at such place or places as the Congress may by law have directed.

Section. 3.

Treason against the United States, shall consist only in levying war against them, or in adhering to their enemies, giving them aid and comfort. No person shall be convicted of treason unless on the testimony of two witnesses to the same overt act, or on confession in open court.

The Congress shall have power to declare the punishment of treason, but no attainder of treason shall work corruption of blood, or forfeiture except during the life of the person attainted.

Article IV.

Section. 1.

Full faith and credit shall be given in each State to the public acts, records, and judicial proceedings of every other State. And the Congress may by general laws prescribe the manner in which such acts, records and proceedings shall be proved, and the effect thereof.

Section. 2.

The citizens of each State shall be entitled to all privileges and immunities of citizens in the several States.

A person charged in any State with treason, felony, or other crime, who shall flee from justice, and be found in another State, shall on demand of the executive authority of the State from which he fled, be delivered up, to be removed to the State having jurisdiction of the crime.

No person held to service or labor in one State, under the laws thereof, escaping into another, shall, in consequence of any law or regulation therein, be discharged from such service or labor, but shall be delivered up on claim of the party to whom such service or labor may be due.

Section. 3.

New States may be admitted by the Congress into this Union; but no new State shall be formed or erected within the jurisdiction of any other State; nor any State be formed by the junction of two or more States, or parts of States, without the consent of the legislatures of the States concerned as well as of the Congress.

The Congress shall have power to dispose of and make all needful rules and regulations respecting the territory or other property belonging to the United States; and nothing in this Constitution shall be so construed as to prejudice any claims of the United States, or of any particular State.

Section. 4.

The United States shall guarantee to every State in this Union a republican form of government, and shall protect each of them against invasion; and on application of the legislature, or of the executive (when the legislature cannot be convened), against domestic violence.

Article V.

The Congress, whenever two-thirds of both houses shall deem it necessary, shall propose Amendments to this Constitution, or, on the application of the legislatures of two-thirds of the several States, shall call a convention for proposing amendments, which, in either case, shall be valid to all Intents and purposes, as part of this Constitution, when ratified by the legislatures of three-fourths of the several States, or by conventions in three-fourths thereof, as the one or the other mode of ratification may be proposed by the Congress; provided that no amendment which may be made prior to the year one thousand eight hundred and eight shall in any manner affect the first and fourth clauses in the ninth section of the first article; and that no State, without its consent, shall be deprived of its equal suffrage in the Senate.

Article VI.

All debts contracted and engagements entered into, before the adoption of this Constitution, shall be as valid against the United States under this Constitution, as under the Confederation.

This Constitution, and the laws of the United States which shall be made in pursuance thereof; and all treaties made, or which shall be made, under the authority of the United States, shall be the supreme law of the land; and the judges in every State shall be bound thereby, any thing in the Constitution or laws of any State to the contrary notwithstanding.

The senators and representatives before mentioned, and the members of the several State legislatures, and all executive and judicial officers, both of the United States and of the several States, shall be bound by oath or affirmation, to support this Constitution; but no religious test shall ever be required as a qualification to any office or public trust under the United States.

Article VII.

The ratification of the conventions of nine States, shall be sufficient for the establishment of this Constitution between the States so ratifying the same.

Done in convention by the unanimous consent of the States present, the seventeenth day of September in the year of our Lord one thousand seven hundred and eighty-seven, and of the independence of the United States of America the twelfth.

Glossary

agent Antifederalists espouse the agent theory of representation. The theory posits that elected officials are responsible for carrying out the wishes of their constituents and that officials are worthy of trust to the extent that and they share with their constituents the same opinions, passions, and interests.

circular letter A circular letter was a document meant to circulate among official bodies or the general public. Papal letters to bishops, called encyclicals (Greek for "in a circle"), were the prototype of circular letters.

Congress The central government operating under the Articles of Confederation was generally referred to as Congress.

ratification Ratification is a formal confirmation by a principal party (e.g., the people) of an action undertaken by an agent (e.g., a convention) and is a prerequisite of final adoption. While often a synonym for acceptance, ratification can also refer to the process of review and thus includes the possibility of nonratification, or rejection.

representative Representative has both a specific and a general meaning. Specifically, it refers to a member of the House of Representatives; generally, it refers to any member of Congress, senators included. In this game the term often encompasses both types of elected officials.

representative democracy Representative democracy was a common definition of a republic at the time. The term *republic*, as employed in this game, usually means a modified form of democracy.

trustee Federalists espouse the trustee theory of representation. The theory posits that elected officials are responsible for enlightening public opinion, not simply reflecting it—the purpose being better deliberation regarding problems of national import.

Credits

TEXT

From THE CREATION OF THE AMERICAN REPUBLIC, 1776–1787 by Gordon S. Wood. Published for the Omohundro Institute of Early American History and Culture. Copyright © 1970 by the University of North Carolina Press; new preface copyright © 1998 by the University of North Carolina Press. Used by permission of the publisher. www.uncpress.org.

PHOTOS

Author Photo: Jim Gibe/Pivot Media, Inc; **p. 10:** WDC Photos/Alamy Stock Photo; **p.12:** MPI/Getty Images; **p.15:** Courtesy of the American Antiquarian Society; **p. 26:** Library of Congress; **p. 27 (top):** Granger; **p. 27 (bottom):** Library of Congress; **p. 28:** Library of Congress; **p. 35:** History and Art Collection/Alamy Stock Photo; **p. 36:** Post Office™ Murals reprinted with the permission of the United States Postal Service. All Rights Reserved. Written authorization from the Postal Service is required to use, reproduce, post, transmit, distribute, or publicly display these images.

Acknowledgments

I wish to thank my student assistant, Faith Keenan of Smith College, who conducted preliminary research on the delegate role descriptions. Also, thanks to the many faculty who used the game in their courses during its development phase, especially Paul Otto of George Fox University. The game was reviewed by the Reacting Editorial Board, and I extend my appreciation to the reviewers: Jace Weaver of University of Georgia, Bill Offutt of Pace University, Scout Blum of Troy University, and Nick Proctor of Simpson College. Finally, thanks to Justin Cahill, editor at W. W. Norton, who shepherded the manuscript through to publication.